United States Office of Education

Historical Summary and Reports

on the systems of public instruction in Spain, Bolivia, Uruguay and

Portugal - Vol. 4

United States Office of Education

Historical Summary and Reports
on the systems of public instruction in Spain, Bolivia, Uruguay and Portugal - Vol. 4

ISBN/EAN: 9783337239473

Printed in Europe, USA, Canada, Australia, Japan

Cover: Foto ©ninafisch / pixelio.de

More available books at **www.hansebooks.com**

CIRCULARS OF INFORMATION

OF THE

BUREAU OF EDUCATIO

No. 1–1873.

HISTORICAL SUMMARY AND REPORTS ON THE SYSTEMS OF PUBLIC INSTRUCTION IN SPAIN, BOLIVIA, URUGUAY, AND PORTUGAL.

WASHINGTON:
GOVERNMENT PRINTING OFFICE.
1873.

CONTENTS.

	Page.
LETTER OF THE COMMISSIONER TO THE SECRETARY OF THE INTERIOR	5
EDUCATION IN SPAIN:	
Introduction	9
History of education in Spain	9
The rule of Sertorius	9
Establishment of the Roman power	10
Spain during the first period of the Roman empire	11
Famous schools and teachers during the first century of the Christian era.	11
Early courses of instruction	12
Intolerance of the Spanish Church	12
Reigns of the first Gothic kings	13
Eminent Christian teachers	13
Invasions by the Vandals, Suevians, and Goths	13
Differences between the Goths and the Spaniards	13
Intolerance toward the Jews	14
Education during the seventh century	14
The invasion of the Moors	16
The reign of Hashem I	16
The reign of Abderrahman II	16
The reign of Mohammed I	17
The reigns of Abderraham III. and Alhakem II	17
Free-schools	18
The reign of Hashem II	18
The reign of Hadshib	19
General character of the Moorish period	19
Moorish view of education	20
The Moorish schools	20
The Christians during the Moorish period	21
Education in the tenth century	21
Foundation of the University of Salamanca	22
The educational efforts of Alphons X	22
Establishment of new academies and universities	23
The discovery of America and its consequences.—The inquisition and the Jesuits	24
Famous scholars of the sixteenth century	25
Attempt at educational reform by Simon Abril	26
State of education during the first half of the eighteenth century	27
State of education during the second half of the eighteenth century	28
The French invasion	29
The constitution of 1812	29
The period of civil wars	30
Recent history, 1845–1873	30
The educational law of 1857	31
Supreme educational authority	32
Provincial and local educational authorities	32
Primary instruction	33

	Page.
EDUCATION IN SPAIN—Continued.	
Statistics	33
Secondary instruction	34
Normal-schools	34
Superior instruction	34
Special instruction	35
EDUCATION IN BOLIVIA:	
Constitutional provisions regarding education	39
History of public instruction	39
Primary instruction	40
Infant-schools	41
Female colleges	41
Secondary instruction	42
Superior instruction	42
Academies of forensic practice	43
Art-colleges	43
Mining-schools	43
Libraries and public museums	43
Agricultural college	44
EDUCATION IN URUGUAY:	
Legal provisions for public instruction	47
Statistics	49
EDUCATION IN PORTUGAL:	
Early history	53
Portugal under the Burgundian dynasty	53
Portugal under the Aviz dynasty, 1385–1580	55
Portugal under Spanish rule, 1581–1640	55
First establishment of the Jesuits in Portugal	55
The reforms of Minister Pombal	56
From Pombal's downfall to the present time	57
Present state of education in Portugal: Primary instruction; course of instruction	59
Attendance at school	60
Want of good text-books	60
Inspection	60
Teachers	61
Night-schools	61
Establishment of new schools	61
Statistics of primary instruction	62
Secondary instruction	62
Superior instruction	64
Special instruction	65

LETTER.

DEPARTMENT OF THE INTERIOR,
BUREAU OF EDUCATION,
Washington, D. C., April, 1873.

SIR: I have the honor to submit the following Reports on Education in various foreign countries, which contain information of interest to educators.

The historical summaries of the educational efforts in Spain and Portugal are considered essential to a correct understanding of their present educational status.

The official reports furnished to this Office by the courtesy of the Brazilian minister have been carefully translated. Their publication seems desirable, as they contain information not otherwise accessible.

The papers herewith submitted consist—

First. Of an Historical Summary of Education in Spain, translated from Schmid's *Educational Cyclopedia.*

Second. Of a Report upon Education in Bolivia, made to the Brazilian government by the Brazilian minister at La Paz, in April, 1872.

Third. Of a Report upon Education in Uruguay, made to the Brazilian government by the Brazilian minister at Montevideo, in March, 1872.

For these two reports I am indebted to Councilor A. P. de Carvalho Borges, envoy extraordinary and minister plenipotentiary of Brazil.

Fourth. Education in Portugal. The historical summary taken from Schmid's *Educational Cyclopedia;* the report on primary education, furnished by Mr. J. C. Rodrigues, editor of *O Novo Mundo,* an illustrated Portuguese journal published in New York; the account of the system of higher instruction is derived from Schmid's *Educational Cyclopedia* and from the official report of the Brazilian minister at Lisbon.

I request your approval of the publication of these papers as a circular of information.

Very respectfully, your obedient servant,

JOHN EATON, JR.,
Commissioner.

Hon. COLUMBUS DELANO,
Secretary of the Interior.

Approved and printing ordered.

C. DELANO,
Secretary of the Interior.

EDUCATION IN SPAIN.

EDUCATION IN SPAIN.

INTRODUCTION.

Spain, after having remained for centuries in a state of lethargy, has, within the past few years, made noticeable progress in general enlightenment and civilization.

That her former state of indifference was not her normal condition, but that on the contrary there are in the Spanish nation elements capable of the highest development, which need only the warming and enlivening sunshine of a wise and liberal government, is shown in the recent reformatory movements, and will be confirmed by a brief review of her educational history during the past ages.

In the following historical summary the excellent article contributed by Professor Le Roy, of the university at Liège, Belgium, to Dr. Schmid's *Educational Cyclopedia** has been chiefly consulted.

HISTORY OF EDUCATION IN SPAIN.

The oldest known inhabitants of the Spanish peninsula were the Iberians. In pre-historic times Celtic nations invaded the country from the north, and after long and sanguinary wars, gradually intermingling and intermarrying with the natives, formed the nation of the Celtiberians. The country was first made known to the rest of the world by the Phenicians, who founded colonies, of which Cadiz was the most important. They were followed by the Greeks, who founded the colony of Saguntum; and the Greeks, in their turn, by the Carthaginians, who founded New Carthage, now Carthagena. During the Punic wars the Carthaginians, who had gradually subjugated the greater part of Spain, were driven out by the Romans, and Spain became, at least in name, a Roman province, for the conquest of the whole peninsula was not completed till A. D. 19.

THE RULE OF SERTORIUS.

In the year 83 B. C., Sertorius, a Roman general, after the first civil war, fled to Spain; with him we may appropriately begin our educational history. Landing in Spain, he found the last scattered remains of the party for which he had fought in Italy. He succeeded in gain-

---

* *Educational Cyclopedia*, (" *Encyclopädie des Erziehungs- und Unterrichtswesens*,") edited by Dr. K. A. Schmid, Rector of the Gymnasium at Stuttgart. 81st part. 1871.

ing the confidence of the native chiefs to such a degree that soon he became the recognized ruler of the country. In order to strengthen his throne and to accustom the natives to a regular form of government, he determined to transplant the Roman institutions to Spain; he formed a Senate of three hundred members, and introduced the military practice of his native country. But this far-seeing man did even more; he assembled in Osca (Huesca in Aragon) a large number of young men of the best families and had them instructed by competent teachers in the science and literature of Greece and Rome. He personally superintended their studies, and from time to time held examinations, at which he awarded prizes to the best scholars. Thus we read in Plutarch that he gladdened the hearts of the fathers, when they saw their sons in their togas lined with purple and the "*bulla*" suspended from the neck. This was the distinction won at school and at the same time a pledge of faithfulness to the benefactor of Spain. It soon, however, became evident that in instituting this school the design of Sertorius was just as much to secure hostages as to raise the standard of education, and a national reaction began to set in, which finally culminated in open revolt. In the suppression of the rebellion Sertorius made himself entirely unpopular, for he let his vengeance fall upon these youths, some of them being killed and others sold as slaves.

ESTABLISHMENT OF THE ROMAN POWER.

If at that time the *Æneid* had been written, the Spaniards might well have applied the "*Timeo Danaos*" to themselves. Perpenna's dagger freed them from the murderer of their children. Perpenna soon had to make way for Pompey, and Rome cast a broader shadow than ever over Spain. But it took all the energy of the last-mentioned general, and finally the terror that preceded Cæsar's arms, to bend underneath the Roman yoke those nations which then, as to-day, imbibed the spirit of provincial independence with their mother's milk. On account of this marked personal independence their revolts were always wanting in unity of purpose, and therefore easily suppressed. The consolidation of the Roman power found, on the other hand, a powerful help in the prevalence of the Latin language, which during the time of the Scipios had first been introduced in Spain, and which after the expulsion of the Carthaginians had spread with incredible ease and rapidity even as far as Bætica, leaving the original idioms to the most inaccessible mountain regions. According to Strabo a Spaniard could scarcely be distinguished from a Roman in the time of Augustus. During the lifetime of Cicero several poets from Corduba were admired in Rome; but this close observer found yet in their pronunciation "*pingue quiddam atque peregrinum*," (something heavy and foreign.) The blending of the two nations became so complete, however, that it may be said without exaggeration that Spain, with the exception perhaps of Galicia and Asturia, which were never completely subjugated, had become the most

Roman of all the provinces of the empire. An allusion to these Cantabrian wars is found in Juvenal, (*Satire* viii,) where he says: "*Horrida vitanda est Hispani*," &c. As regards the portions bordering on the Mediterranean, especially Andalusia, Roman influence became all-powerful; as a direct consequence of this influence a large number of Spaniards came to Rome every year, and, as the Greeks had done before them, surpassed their conquerors on the field of literature and science.

SPAIN DURING THE FIRST PERIOD OF THE ROMAN EMPIRE.

Latin eloquence declined in Italy from the first days of the empire; natural eloquence was supplanted by rhetorical trickery. Poetry shone in its greatest splendor during the reign of Augustus. It was a reflection of the bright light that had been kindled in Greece, but during the reign of Tiberius it lost its natural beauty and its serene gracefulness; men of deeper thought sought refuge in stoic philosophy, while the governing power found its chief support in the thoughtless multitude. It flattered their insatiable desire for sensual enjoyments, and built the Coliseum, the true temple of Cæsarism. It is a fact worthy of note that in those times of trials, of terrors, and of insane orgies, Spaniards represented in Rome the spirit of old Rome; and the accession to the throne of two Spanish nobles, Trajan and Hadrian, once more arrested the fatal course of the empire hurrying to destruction, and made a brief but brilliant era in the history of Roman art and literature.

FAMOUS SCHOOLS AND TEACHERS DURING THE FIRST CENTURY OF THE CHRISTIAN ERA.

The schools of Corduba seem to have been particularly flourishing during the first century of the Christian era. From these schools there came to Rome the orator M. Porcius Latro, among whose pupils were men like Augustus, Mæcenas, Agrippa, and Ovid; his intimate friend M. Annæus Seneca, the father of the philosopher, and L. Annæus Seneca himself, whose teacher was Hyginus, likewise (at least according to the best authorities) a Corduban. Seneca's nephew Lucan was educated in Rome, but indirectly he was, through the intercourse with his uncle, under a strong Spanish influence. The poet Sextilius Henna, the public reader Victorius Statorius, and many others of less note might be mentioned, but they all fade away before more famous names, which show how far education had spread throughout the whole of Spain. Quintilian, the author of excellent educational works, and of the most complete treatise on rhetoric among the ancients, was a native of Calagurris, (Calahorra in the present Spanish province of Logroño.) It is well known how successful he was as a teacher of eloquence, first in Spain and afterward in Rome, but it is perhaps less generally known that he was the first who drew a salary as such from the government. Martial, the epigrammatist, born at Bilbilis, (Calatayud in the present province of Saragossa;) Columella, the agronomic writer from Cadiz;

Pomponius Mela, the geographer, from the neighborhood of Mellaria in Bætica; Silius Italicus, the poet; Florus, the compiler; Antonius Julianus, and Herennius Senecio, the scholars of Quintilian; and finally Voconius, the friend of the younger Pliny. As a man of learning and patron of the sciences and arts, the Emperor Hadrian may likewise claim a place among the famous names. Stars of the first magnitude were rare among the constellations of the empire, but it must be borne in mind that the golden age was irrevocably past. The language of Cicero had lost more of its original purity and elegance in Spain than in Italy, and many of her later writers excelled in nothing but a bombastic style—an artificial, exaggerated mode of expression; in highflown essays on insignificant subjects; in the affected severity of the stoics, which but little agrees with a refined æsthetic feeling. But in spite of this it is nevertheless true that the Spaniards have a great share in the literary *renaissance*, which characterizes the period between the reign of Vespasian and the time of the Antonines.

EARLY COURSES OF INSTRUCTION.

Columella's book *De re rustica* was introduced into the Spanish schools as a text-book, and thus a real course of agriculture was combined with instruction in grammar, rhetoric, and law. During the reigns of the later emperors these studies assumed more and more a cyclopedic character, of which the work of the elder Pliny is a striking example; the same, but in another direction, may be said also of the *Institutiones* of Quintilian. At this time shorter text-books, epitomized from larger works, were introduced.

The social change had also produced new wants; attention was dispersed over a large number of subjects; a certain variety of knowledge, even though superficial, had become a necessity for an educated man, and, as is always the case in nations that have passed their meridian height, and are approaching a state of dissolution, mere booklearning was esteemed more highly than true genius.

INTOLERANCE OF THE SPANISH CHURCH.

The introduction of Christianity did not bear any fruit till the downfall of the Roman empire. Even during the early ages the Spanish Church had her martyrs, for scarcely did she feel herself master in her dominion when in her annals we find an act of intolerance: the beheading of Priscillian, the heretic, A. D. 385, at the instigation of the bishops Ithacus and Idacus. It must, however, be mentioned in honor of the Spanish clergy at that time that this act produced the greatest indignation against the two bishops. The Spanish clergy were not as yet animated by the sanguinary religious zeal which in later centuries became one of their characteristics.

REIGNS OF THE FIRST GOTHIC KINGS.

New trials were in store for the Spanish Church during the reigns of the first Gothic kings, who were Arians. But when the period of forced tolerance came to an end, when Leovigild and Reccared had been converted to the orthodox Roman Catholic faith, the Church amply indemnified itself. Royalty in Spain, more than in any other country, had a religious character, and the doctrine of the "worldly arm" was there carried out to its fullest extent. It is but natural that all public institutions, and the education of youth more so than any other, should have felt this change.

EMINENT CHRISTIAN TEACHERS.

The early Spanish Christians had several eminent teachers and educators. Religious poetry was also in high favor among them, and men like Juvencus, Rufus, Festus, Aquilius Severus, and, above all, Prudentius, the opponent of Symmachus, deserve to be mentioned. As historian Orosius distinguished himself. How far already do we seem to be from the century of a Lucan, a Seneca, a Quintilian! But the darkness was to become still more dense.

INVASIONS BY THE VANDALS, SUEVIANS, AND GOTHS.

Effeminated by a long period of peace, the Spaniards were not able to defend themselves against the Vandals, who invaded the peninsula and cruelly devastated it for two years. They were followed by the Suevians, who finished the work of devastation. Many cities were entirely destroyed, and their inhabitants cruelly murdered. Spain had scarcely begun to recover, when the Visigoths made their appearance, just as warlike, but, fortunately, less savage than their predecessors. It is true that they likewise murdered and devastated, but they built up again, and their social institutions were far superior to those of the other invading nations.

DIFFERENCES BETWEEN THE GOTHS AND THE SPANIARDS.

As long as the Goths remained Arians there existed a broad gulf between the conquerors and the conquered. Beside this they were entirely different in natural disposition, language, historical traditions, and even in dress. The Spaniards, of middle size, with bronzed faces and black eyes, formed a striking contrast to the sons of the north with their tall, powerful figures, blue eyes, and light complexion. The former spoke Latin, wore the toga, and had their hair cut short; the latter spoke the language of Ulfilas, wore furs, and would have considered themselves dishonored if their heads had been deprived of any hair. The Spaniards had the law of Theodosius; the Goths had no written laws whatever, and hence considered skill in arms the only desirable object, while the Spaniards had an appreciation of arts and sciences. The irresistible power of mental superiority was so great that the Gothic kings soon discovered that in the appointments to important official positions they would have to look chiefly to the Romans if their social fabric was to rest on any secure foundations. The real amalgamation of the races, however, did not begin till religious faith no longer formed a dividing line, and when the Visigothic law, at last written and codified and supplemented from the Theodosian code and the canons of the national council, could be introduced among the whole nation.

Guizot has made the remark that the legislation of the Visigoths, in contradistinction to those of other barbarous nations, was "real" and not "personal;" *i. e.*, based on the landed estate and not on the nationality of those who were made subject to it. In the introduction of this civilizing principle of the equality of men before the law, he justly sees the influence of the "philosophers of those ages," viz, the clergy. The revival of civilization in Spain was largely due to the predominance of the theocratic priciple. This ascendency of mental and moral over mere brute force was certainly beneficial, but it had also its dark side. The kings, guided by the clergy, introduced numerous measures tending to mental progress and to milder customs, with one exception: religious intolerance was legally sanctified and raised to the blindest fanaticism; and the fact cannot be denied that this traditionary policy, which has been followed during all the successive governments, and which, even at the present day, has not yet been entirely rooted out, has been the chief cause of the political decline and the misfortunes of Spain.

INTOLERANCE TOWARD THE JEWS.

The inexorable rigor of the inquisition in later years was foreshadowed by the cruelty with which the Visigothic laws treated the Jews, and in the persecutions which King Sisebut, an otherwise moderate man, instituted against this unfortunate race. The cruelties practiced were so great that the Council of Toledo condemned them, but without making any redress. The consequence was that many Jews emigrated, and the temper of those who remained became so embittered that they openly assisted the Moors in their invasion of Andalusia.

EDUCATION DURING THE SEVENTH CENTURY.

It can easily be imagined that the troubles of the fifth century, and the invasion of the Goths, dealt a deadly blow to education; the clergy alone kept its lamp burning in the midst of the dense darkness. Three names especially deserve to be mentioned, the three brothers Leander, Fulgentius, and Isidorus, of Sevilla, in the seventh century; all three· well versed in Hebrew, Greek, and Latin literature. Isidorus wrote a work entitled the *Etymologicon*, (*Originum, sive Etymologiarum, libri* xx,) a real cyclopedia of useful knowledge. This work, left unfinished by him, was completed by Bishop Braulio, of Saragossa, and was used as a text-book till the twelfth century. The table of contents will give some idea of the work: Book 1. Grammar and history. 2. Rhetoric and dialectics. 3. Arithmetic, geometry, astronomy, and music. 4. Medicine. 5. Law. 6. Book-copyists and clerical offices. 7. Of God. 8. Of the church and synagogue, heresies, schisms, sorcerers, and heathen. 9. Of languages. 10. Etymologies, alphabetically arranged. 11. Of man. 12. Of animals. 13 and 14. Of the world and the universe. 15. Of towns, houses, and landed estates. 16. Of metals, stones, weights, and measures. 17. Of agriculture and horticulture. 18. War and games. 19. Architecture, naval affairs, clothing. 20. Food and various household utensils.

Bishop Braulio studied natural history, but his work on this subject only shows how low the schools of those days had sunk. It cannot be denied that the clergy were intent on saving the threatened civilization. But their aim was exclusively a religious one, and science had in their opinion only value in so far as it served as an aid for the studies of the clergy. The chief object was to influence the barbarians so far as to accept the civilizing doctrines of Christianity, and in order to further this end a more orderly state of society had to be organized, and the Church, at that time the only keeper and guardian of science, could only appreciate that social condition in which *she* was to be all-powerful. Her natural aim was to insure the complete victory of spirit over matter. She alone was able to pave the way for this victory, and she was conscious of this. Hence her care for the education of a spiritual army, and the resolution of the Second Council of Toledo, according to which those young men, who by their parents were destined for the Church, were confided to the care of priests located in those cities where bishops had their seats. But all this did not constitute a proper school. In order to become a priest or bishop, it was not necessary to have any general education; all that was required was to be acquainted with the Holy Scriptures, the rules of discipline, and the ceremonies of divine worship. If any of the scholars showed special talents, the bishops endeavored to give them a better education. With regard to the instruction which, during the reign of the Visigoths, was given to the mass of the children, history is silent; it is, however, supposed that there existed a course in catechism for them, because a decree of the Council of Toledo, of the year 694, ordered the children of Jews, when they had reached the age of seven years, to be taken from their parents in order that they might be instructed in the Christian religion.

Gradually the Gothic kings had begun to take pleasure in mental improvement; they commenced to protect and favor authors, had rare manuscripts copied, and increased their libraries considerably; but the sudden invasion of the Moors brought all their plans to a premature end, and on the ruins of the Gothic kingdom founded an empire which, as soon as it was firmly established, took a pride beyond all else in furthering science, art, and literature, on a new and totally different basis.

THE INVASION OF THE MOORS.

In direct opposition to the Germanic nations, the Moors were prompted to their conquering expeditions by religious zeal. Instead of allowing themselves to be converted by the conquered people, they advanced everywhere, "the sword in one hand and the Koran in the other;" they were, however, conscious of the fact that violent measures, in matters of conscience, would be fraught with danger for their empire. Thus the Christians were permitted to live undisturbed at Cordova, and could freely worship according to their religion, with the only condition that they would show respect to Mohammedanism. The church- and convent-schools were not closed, but public offices were given to Mohammedans exclusively; intermarriage between Christians and Mohammedans were formed, and the marked advantage and benefits accruing to renegades quietly spread Mohammed's doctrines wherever the Moorish empire extended. The treatment of the Jews was as mild as that of the Christians. In order to establish their empire more firmly the Moors chiefly relied on their own mental superiority and on that material welfare which they brought to every country they conquered. Already in their eastern home they had become acquainted with the writings of the Greeks, and although many of these writings had become tabooed as dangerous to the religious belief of the faithful, Aristotle, Theophrastus, Euclid, Ptolemæus, and Hippocrates were well known in Damascus and Bagdad. When Cordova had become the center of an independent empire, it became heir to the rich mental heritage of the above-mentioned eastern capital, which, after the glorious reigns of Harun-al-Rashid and Almamun, (762–833,) soon began to decline and became a prey to effeminate and demoralizing luxury.

THE REIGN OF HASHEM I.

The second caliph of the Moorish empire in Spain, Hashem I, the contemporary of Harun, initiated the age of modern mental development. He protected men of learning, and founded schools to which Christians were admitted and were taught Arabic, a measure which tended largely to bring the two nations into closer contact.

THE REIGN OF ABDERRAHMAN II.

Abderrahman II. continued the work of his predecessor. The schools, in a large number of cities, were liberally endowed from the government treasury; three hundred orphans were boarded and educated, free, in the school connected with the great mosque at Cordova. The caliph was an enthusiastic admirer of poetry, and his own impromptu poems were highly praised. He was very fond of music, and, by the most liberal offers, induced the famous Persian musician, Ali-ben-Serrab, to come to Spain and found a school of music at Cordova. Magnificent buildings rose everywhere, palaces, mosques, bridges, aqueducts, baths, and fountains; the arrangements for watering the plain of Cordova, carried out on the most gigantic scale, spread fertility and happiness, and made the capital of Andalusia an earthly paradise. The court set an example of refined and elegant living, and mental enjoyments alternated with chivalrous games and festivals of every kind.

THE REIGN OF MOHAMMED I.

Mohammed I., the son and successor of Abderrahman II., showed less zeal in the cause of arts and sciences than his father. But the movement had begun and took its natural course of progress. In Cordova, the house of the learned Jahje-el-Laithi, who in his youth had twice traveled in the East, and who, by his teacher, the famous Malik-ben-Anes, was called "the mind of Spain," and "the wise Andalusian," was thronged by scholars from far and near, like the lecture-hall of a public university.

THE REIGNS OF ABDERRAHMAN III. AND ALHAKEM II.

During the reigns of Abderrahman III. (912–971) and Alhakem II. (971–976) the Moorish empire in Spain reached its zenith of glory and splendor in every respect. Never before had men of learning, poets, and artists enjoyed such favor; never before had larger sums been expended for libraries and scientific collections of every kind. Abderrahman III., who was a man of the highest attainments, succeeded in inspiring his whole court with his own love of knowledge. The house of his grand-vizier, Abu-Aamir-ben-Achmed-ben-Said, became the rendezvous of all the famous men of the empire; poets there read their works, and important scientific questions were discussed as in our academies. Medicine, natural sciences, mathematics, and astronomy were the favorite studies. Alhakem II. crowned his father's work by having fine copies made of all the works of the best ancient and modern writers, (his library is said to have contained upward of 400,000 volumes,) by inducing men of learning from Spain and foreign countries to settle at Cordova, and by protecting the philosophers, who could not now pursue their studies in peace without fear of being murdered by religious fanatics. As a matter of course the schools, under such enlightened rulers, were in a very flourishing condition, and education of all grades was thoroughly organized. Abderrahman even established high-schools for girls. The scholars in these schools were under the care of female teachers, who instructed them in general knowledge and explained the works of the poets to them. Alhakem's care for education extended to all ages and to all classes of society. The primary schools were, according to trustworthy authorities, numerous and excellent. In Andalusia it was very difficult to find a person who could not read and write, while in Christian Europe the highest classes of society, unless they were in the service of the Church, were utterly ignorant in this respect. Grammar and rhetoric were also taught in the schools.

FREE SCHOOLS.

Still, Alhakem was of the opinion that education was not yet sufficiently general; he therefore established in Cordova twenty-seven schools, where children of indigent parents were instructed free of charge, and paid the teachers out of his own private treasury. The University of Cordova in those times was the best in the whole world. In the great mosque—for there the lectures were delivered—Abu-Bekr-ibn-Moawijah lectured on the learned questions regarding Mohammed's person and doctrine; Abu-Ali-Káli, from Bagdad, lectured on the ancient Moors. His course of lectures, which he afterward published himself under the title *Amáli, i. e.*, Dictations, contained an almost incredible mass of the most interesting facts concerning the history of the ancient Moors, their proverbs, their language, and their poetry. Grammar was taught by Ibn-el-Kutiah, who was justly considered the most learned grammarian of Spain. Other sciences were represented by no less famous professors. The number of students was several thousand. Most of them studied what was called "*Fikh*," *i. e.*, theology and law, for this knowledge formed the stepping-stone to the best offices in the government.

THE REIGN OF HASHEM II.

Not only Cordova, but also Granada, Sevilla, Xativa, Valencia, Jaen, Murcia, Almeria, Malaga, Velez, in the tenth century had academies and high-schools which were opened for Christians and Jews as well as for Mohammedans. The Jews had at the same time established special schools for the study of their sacred writings. The model of all these schools was the Jewish academy at Cordova, founded by Rabbi Mosheh, a native of Persia, whose fame attracted many learned men from North Africa, and even from distant parts of Asia. Hashem II., the son of Alhakem II., took the Jews under his special protection, had the Talmud translated into Arabic, and himself took instruction in the Mishnah, (the first part of the Talmud.) The exact sciences were studied with equal zeal by the Jews and by the Moors; all barriers had fallen, and people of the most widely differing religious creeds lived peaceably together, united and protected by a spirit of religious tolerance almost unexampled in history. This state of affairs did not last long, but its beneficial effects could be felt amid those political storms which shook the throne of the caliphs to its very foundation. This was the reason why Hebrew learning and Hebrew literature did not reach its greatest height till the twelfth century, the century of Abenesra and Maimonides. But the influence of religious fanaticism, which, since the usurpation of Hádshib-Almansur began to grow strong in Spain, was so great, that the writings of Maimonides, who otherwise in his views showed himself far ahead of his time, are full of the most bitter hatred against all persons of different religious faith from his own. Almansur, toward the end of the tenth century, initiated the period of reaction, by publicly burning all the literary treasures which Alhakem had collected, with the exception of the theological, grammatical, and medical works. Philosophy was the special object of persecution, but, as Renan truly remarks, " all the efforts to suppress it only gave it new life." The golden age of Alhakem has left no famous names to posterity, but the names of men like Avempace, Abubacer, Avenzoar, and Averroes, who were hunted down by religious maniacs, are inscribed in letters of gold on the true roll of human fame.

THE REIGN OF HADSHIB.

It is but just to say that the intolerance of Hadshib was chiefly caused by a desire to gain the popular favor, in order to maintain himself on his usurped throne. Personally he esteemed men of learning, and historians tell us that in times of peace his palace resembled an academy. He took pleasure in visiting schools and academies, took a seat among the scholars, and did not allow the lesson to be interrupted by his appearance. He generously rewarded the zeal of scholars and teachers, and took great care only to have the best and most learned men appointed as priests and judges. But the civil wars and the conflict with the Christians, which broke out at his death, paralyzed all those efforts for education of which he had been the last promoter. Even as late as the twelfth century Arabic and Jewish science had some famous representatives, but the blight of religious intolerance killed most of its fruits, and the Christian nations were destined to mature the seed of ancient learning. It seems to have been the historic mission of Mohammedanism to preserve the rich inheritance of antiquity through the Dark Ages,* and to transmit it safely to Christian civilization.

GENERAL CHARACTER OF THE MOORISH PERIOD.

The genius of the Moorish nation showed itself on the one hand in its most brilliant colors in poems and romances, in a play of fancy, and in proverbs which contained their code of social morality, and on the other hand in natural sciences, especially chemistry and botany, and in algebra, astronomy, and medicine. It may suffice to mention in this place, that Jews from Cordova carried the science of Avicenna beyond the Pyrenees, and became the principal founders of the famous school of Montpellier. The predominating characteristic of the Moorish scholars consisted in an extreme subtilty, which, applied to religious questions, showed itself in all manner of caviling discussions, particularly after the writings of Aristotle had made them acquainted with the strictly formal method and with a system of metaphysics which exactly suited their minds. Thus they prepared the way for scholasticism, and, having themselves become slaves to an immovable formalism, set a dangerous example to their Christian neighbors. Their influence in this respect has been felt far beyond the Spanish peninsula, and it has cost a long struggle for many of the Christian nations to free themselves from this influence. Science and life were with them two entirely and strictly separate spheres, and the last cause of their irremediable mental barrenness was the fact that, in their religion, and even in their purely lyric poetry, there was wanting that vivifying breath of the spirit which forms the true essence and strength of Christianity, that deep longing for harmony between heaven and earth, between faith and science, which has been the great motor of the Christian nations, and which has finally freed them from the heavy bonds of the Middle-Ages. The Moors, too, have had their middle-ages, but after those had passed they again sank down to the same level as in the times of Mohammed.

MOORISH VIEW OF EDUCATION.

The best idea of their educational views may be gained from the *Proverbs of Meidani*, which treat of filial affection, obedience, the advantages of silence, the value of experience, &c. Only one proverb praises woman: "A virtuous woman leads to all that is great." The reverse, however, follows immediately: "Women are the devil's fishing-nets." But if one looks for actual educational theories, very little is found in the whole of Moorish literature, with the exception of the famous philosophical novel by Ibn-Tofail, of Wadi-Jâsh, (Guadiz,) entitled *Chai ibn Jakdhân, i. e.*, "The living one, the son of the waking one," which, though not quite justly, has been compared to Rousseau's *Emile* and to Defoe's *Robinson Crusoe*. A better comparison would be with Bonnet's *Essai analytique sur les facultés de l'âme*. The author describes the different grades of mental development in a man who has been entirely isolated from human society, but who, through the exertions of his own mind, and through the force of his own reasoning, obtains the knowledge of the mysteries of nature and the highest metaphysical speculations. It is like a dim dawn of the psychological method which, in modern times, has been applied to education, but it is by no means a system of education.

THE MOORISH SCHOOLS.

The elementary schools were connected with the mosques. In these schools reading, writing, and grammar were taught, ancient and modern poems were read, and the Koran was learned by heart. The course of instruction in the academies embraced theology, law, natural sciences, and medicine. In the beginning any one who pleased acted as professor; the lectures were open to all, and free of charge; only some teachers received pay from their scholars, and this was entirely optional. But in course of time the government took the matter in hand, and appointed the teachers and professors.

THE CHRISTIANS DURING THE MOORISH PERIOD.

During the whole Moorish period the Spanish patriots, few in number, but possessed of indomitable courage, carried on an unceasing warfare against the foreign invaders, and gradually succeeded in establishing Christian kingdoms in the northern part of the peninsula. It was as glorious a struggle as any we read of in history, an heroic war whose Iliad is the *Romancero*. " To fight and to sing," these two words contain the whole history of Christian Spain during the Middle Ages, and its representative is the Cid Ruy Diaz de Vivar, el Cid Campeador. This state of affairs was not congenial to the cultivation of the arts and sciences, and the Christian portion of Spain for a long time remained as ignorant as it was heroic. The children, with the exception of those who were shut up in convents, were almost exclusively instructed in the use of arms. The constantly recurring necessity of defending the frontiers prevented the establishment of a settled central government. Nowhere in Europe was in those times the personal freedom of the lower orders and local privileges as great as in Spain. On the other hand, there were frequent infringements on the liberties of the people by the arrogant nobility, causing internal dissensions, and even at times leading to alliances with the Moors, who, since the death of Almansur, were divided into numerous opposing factions. The only places of refuge open to science were the convents, whose inmates took no part in the wars, but many of these, founded by superstition, had become nurseries of indolence, effeminacy, and immorality.

EDUCATION IN THE TENTH CENTURY.

In the tenth century we find only one man of learning worthy of notice, Haiton, bishop of Vich or Ossuna, the mathematical instructor of the famous Gerbert, (afterward Pope Sylvester II.,) who, it is said, introduced the use of Arabic figures into France. Very gradually, however, in proportion as the Christians gained upon the Moors, the greater public security allowed men of science to follow its pursuit more undisturbedly, Several causes concurred in furthering this movement: The growing fame of scholastic philosophy in the convents; the constantly increasing fame of the Paris University, whither large numbers of eager students came from all parts of Spain, as well as from Britain, to enter the ranks of the realists and nominalists, always ready for the fray; the great importance attributed to the Moorish commentaries of Aristotle, and their varied scientific works; the constant intercourse by letter kept up between the graduates of the Paris University who had returned to their homes ; and finally the establishment of the Dominican order, which in a short time spread throughout the greater portion of Western Europe, and which became a nursery of learned theologians and valiant knights of the spirit. The founder of the order was himself a Spaniard, born in Calahorra, 1170, from the noble family at Guzman, who had spent nine years at the famous school of Palencia, at that time the first in Castile. The dawn of a new era had begun, but the circumstance which more than any other tended toward a revival of learning in Spain was the transfer of the school of Palencia to Salamanca.

FOUNDATION OF THE UNIVERSITY OF SALAMANCA.

The first foundation of the University of Salamanca dates as far back as the year 1200, during the reign of Alphons IX. But the transfer mentioned above seems, according to the most trustworthy historians, not to have taken place till the reign of Ferdinand III., (1295–1312.) The new university had in the beginning to contend with great difficulties; it possessed great privileges, but very little money, and the professors had no fixed salary. In the year 1250, Alphons X. granted an annual sum of 2,500 maravedis,* for the professors' salaries; and still we find that, after a short period of splendor, the university, about 1310, had again sunk into insignificance; only several years later it became a university of the first rank, and the rival of Paris, Oxford, and Bologna.

THE EDUCATIONAL EFFORTS OF ALPHONS X.

Too great praise cannot be bestowed on Alphons X. (Alonzo el Sabio,) for his zeal in the cause of education and science. Before his reign the professorships were almost exclusively theological, while he also established professorships of the sciences. Under his directions did the professors of Salamanca compose the famous *Alphonsic Tables*, (astronomical tables;) they translated the works of Avicenna, Averroes, and of the commentators of Galenus; they assisted in editing the famous collection of laws, well known under the title *Las siete partidas*, which contains an extremely interesting chapter on the *Estudios generales*, (Part II., tit. 31.) One finds there laws and regulations of the greatest wisdom, which partly have been adopted by the universities of other countries and have been retained to this day. At the head of the University of Salamanca there was a rector who remained in office for one year, and was usually a member of one of the first families of the country. The rector, after consulting with the academic council, consisting of all the professors, filled vacant professorships. The university judiciary, to which all graduates and students were subject, was till 1334 in the hands of the bishop of the diocese, who in his functions was assisted by several other dignitaries of the Church; it was in the above-mentioned year transferred to a special official, the *maestrescuela*. The university comprised schools of all grades. In the *escuelas mayores* the course of instruction embraced: Theology, ecclesiastical and civil law, mathematics, natural

---

* Equivalent at that period to about $12,000 present value.

philosophy, moral philosophy, languages and rhetoric; in the *escuelas menores: las artes y canones*, grammar, and music; in the *escuelas minimas*: the elements of grammar. These schools were all located in three magnificent buildings, of which two stand even now and serve the same purpose. Numerous colleges rose gradually by the side of the *alma mater*, and Salamanca swarmed with monks of different orders and with students, all passionately fond of sharp scholastic disputations; some of the Spanish novelists have given us vivid descriptions of the life and manners of these old Spanish students. Salamanca at this period had about ten thousand students; at the end of the sixteenth century there were about six thousand; about the middle of the eighteenth century their number was one thousand, and at present it is about five hundred. The fame of the university was so great that at the time of the great schism of Avignon, (1378-1429,) the two Popes, Urban and Clement, asked the advice of the learned doctors of Salamanca and willingly submitted to their decision. Columbus also submitted to them his great plans of discovery. As an instance of the liberal spirit prevailing at this university, it deserves to be mentioned that there the system of Copernicus was taught early in the beginning of the sixteenth century, at a time when everywhere else it was considered heretical. Such boldness, however, was of no long duration in a university where, in the conferring of degrees, the papal and royal authorities had equal influence. Nowhere was so much time lost in barren discussions, and nowhere was the art of distilling abstract ideas, without leaving a certain narrow circle, so well understood as at Salamanca. Durandus and Scotus were the beginning and the end of all philosophy, and innumerable theologians and priests argued in a noisy manner, without finding any admirers but their own teachers. In the time of Charles V., we find a few names of note like Covarrubias and De Soto, but after these nothing but hopeless mediocrity. There was, however, no lack of Spaniards who were true disciples of science, and from the thirteenth century we find them at many Italian universities; the famous Cardinal Carillo de Albornoz, in the year 1365, founded for them at Bologna the College of San Clemente, which has been in existence till our days. This mutual relation between Spain and Italy proved very beneficial to both countries. As an instance we may mention the famous humanist Antonio de Lebrixa, (Nebrissensis,) who was educated in Bologna, was professor of the Latin language in Salamanca for twenty years, and gave to his native country its first dictionary and grammar.

ESTABLISHMENT OF NEW ACADEMIES AND UNIVERSITIES.

It would lead us too far to enumerate here all the academies and high schools which were established in Spain till the end of the Middle-Ages. There is one fact, however, regarding Catalonia, which is of interest. Jaïme II., the founder of the University of Lerida, (Ilerdensis,) in vain issued decrees forbidding the other cities of his dominions to establish superior institutions of learning; the force of circumstances compelled him to make one concession after the other. In Valencia the city authorities founded a university in spite of the most violent resistance of the bishop. The same object was accomplished in Barcelona, in 1450. But this spirit of emulation bore scarcely any fruit; and it may be said that Spain was never so near its mental decadence than just at the time when it seemed to have reached the very pinnacle of power, and when it was literally true that the sun never set in the empire of Charles V.

THE DISCOVERY OF AMERICA AND ITS CONSEQUENCES.—THE INQUISITION AND THE JESUITS.

The discovery of America, the establishment of the inquisition, the expulsion of the Jews, and more than all this, the foundation of the order of the Jesuits, created for Spain a very peculiar position, which formed a very striking contrast to that of all the other civilized nations of Europe at that period. Gold and silver in unheard-of quantities flowed into the public treasury from the American mines; the consequence was a more and more despotic system of government, as the kings were no longer obliged to call the Cortes together in order to raise money. The immense increase of private wealth only tended to increase the natural indolence of the Spaniards. People went to the Indies (America) in order quickly to grow rich, the resources of the mother-country were neglected, and the great mass of the people plunged wildly into luxury and immorality. At no time was education so much neglected. Young people left to themselves from the fifteenth or sixteenth year of age, lived in a state of complete idleness and even boasted of their extravagance. This is one of the causes of the depopulation of the kingdom. No less baneful was the influence of the inquisition. The Moors and Jews took their science and their industry with them into their banishment, and in bigoted and indolent Spain there remained only persecuting monks and priests, brutal soldiers, adventurers, and beggars. Cardinal Ximenes made great exertions to revive a scientific spirit by founding the University of Alcala, (Complutensis,) in the year 1504, the foundation of whose fame was laid at once by the edition of the famous polyglot Bible, and which, during the second half of the sixteenth century, when Cervantes studied there, shone with greater splendor than all the other Spanish universities. But outside of the sporadic works of a small number of learned men, and perhaps five or six great poets and prose-writers, Spain, which once possessed all the requirements to become the first nation of the world, gradually sank down to the very lowest grade on the scale of European civilization. What sphere could be found for liberty of thought and noble aims in a country where *autos-da-fé* were great national festivals? Those who aimed at something higher and better studied in Italy, and frequently remained there. The victories and the policy of Charles V. had here likewise established the Spanish supremacy, but the sun of science and art continued to shine in Italy with incomparable splendor, and the inquisition never took such deep root there as on the Spanish peninsula. The Dominicans and the universities did, in the beginning, by no means look favorably on the establishment of Jesuit colleges in the chief cities of the kingdom. Charles V. never trusted the Jesuits, and Philip II. said, "The only order which I do not understand is the order of the Jesuits;" but in spite of this they pursued their aims with patience and perseverance. Before fifty years had passed they were masters of the situation, through the intimate bond connecting them directly with the Roman pontiff, by the principle of passive obedience (*perinde ac cadaver*) laid down in their constitution, and by the influence which, through preaching, confession, and the education of youth, they had obtained over all classes of society. It must be granted that with regard to education they possess real merits; they improved the method of instruction in the classic languages, and their prudent discipline did not fail to exercise a salutary reaction against the growing licentiousness. These results, however, were more external and seeming than lasting and real. The casuistry in Mariana's book *De rege*, (written for the instruction of the crown-prince;) the subtilties of Sanchez, Escobar, and Caramuel, cannot easily be reconciled with the spirit of the Gospel. Especially in Spain and in South America have the doctrines of the Jesuits, as applied to education, paralyzed liberal thought. The Jesuits let the inquisition exterminate the heretics with fire and sword, while they themselves carried on the warfare with the arms of dialectics and science. After having become reconciled to the *Santo Officio* they took possession of all the schools, and finally also of the universities. The inquisition prohibited all suspicious books, and the Jesuits confined free thought in constantly narrowing circles. Absolute ignorance held full sway in philosophy, history, the exact sciences, and in the mechanical arts. Since the middle of the sixteenth century there were in Spain no more engineers, the art of printing declined, and the gold of both the Indies went to foreign countries without any benefit to the mother-country. The Jesuit colleges were not wanting in admirable arrangements, but the rations of knowledge, so to speak, were measured out to the pupils in accordance with the aims pursued by the order. The study of grammar and rhetoric was flourishing; Latin odes and elegies were composed by the pupils, the logic of Aristotle was explained, and much time was devoted to argue trivial questions in a skillful manner, but everything was superficial and without real benefit. The ideal aimed at was a complete Jesuit, not a man in the full sense of the word. In Paraguay the experiment was carried out fully.

FAMOUS SCHOLARS OF THE SIXTEENTH CENTURY.

The indirect influence of some scholars of this period contributed a little to the further development of science, if not to the general education of the people. Among those who deserve special mention there is

Juan Luiz Vives, a somewhat dry but very learned writer, worthy of being placed by the side of Erasmus and Budæus. His books, *De ratione studii puerilis, De tradendis disciplinis, De causis corruptarum artium,* deserve a place in every history of education, but they were not written in Spain. The grammarian F. Sanchez, (Sanctius,) who in his native country was called *el doctor de todos los hombres de letras,* and *el padre de la lengua latina,* during the reign of Philip II. wrote an admirable work, *Minerva, sive de causis linguæ latinæ,* which formed the basis of the *Méthode latine* of the humanists of Port Royal. Another important work was the *Examen de los ingenios para las ciencias,* written by Huarte in 1580; and, finally, we cannot pass over in silence the works of Pedro de Ponce, who was the first inventor of a method of instruction for the deaf and dumb. But all these are only isolated examples, and in passing from the sixteenth to the seventeenth century we see nothing but the most deplorable decline of science. In order to find a revival of scientific studies we must go as far as the accession of the Bourbons to the throne of Spain.

ATTEMPT AT EDUCATIONAL REFORM BY SIMON ABRIL.

A Spanish journalist, M. J. M. Guardia, living in France, has, some years ago, brought to light a remarkable memorial on the reform of education, which Dr. Pedro Simon Abril, professor of the Greek language at the University of Saragossa, in the year 1589 addressed to Philip II. It was a bold step of the worthy doctor, but by addressing himself directly to the king he showed his wisdom, for this was the surest way of quieting clerical censure. He obtained nothing by it, but his is the honor of having attempted a reform; and his memorial is of great historical interest, for in bringing forward his thoughts of reform he points out the weak sides of the system, and gives us a striking picture of the Spanish schools under the rule of the blindest despotism. The government sent from time to time official inspectors, whose duty it was to correct abuses which might have crept in in course of time. But, as Dr. Abril says, they did not busy themselves with educational questions, and examined only the food and clothing of the scholars. Simon Abril insists on the necessity of paying attention to the method of instruction, and compares the old and new methods. He urgently demands that teachers should no longer use the Latin language in giving instruction; he complains of the vagueness of the subjects assigned to the different professors; of the impatience of the students, who in their haste to obtain degrees acquire a very superficial knowledge, and do not take the time and trouble to study the great authors of antiquity; the reform of the whole system of education ought to be delayed no longer. He says, "Let us begin with the beginning; why is not the grammar of our mother-tongue taught in the smaller (primary) schools, and why are our grammars written in Latin; why are meaningless rules learned by heart instead of storing the child's mind with useful moral axioms, as was the custom in former times, when the rules were learned by studying various authors; why these endless translations into a foreign language instead of translations from foreign languages?" He is also dissatisfied with instruction in logic, and with regard to this he says: "Logic in itself is of no value; it is only valuable by the use which is made of it; it is a tool to work with, and no more; people break their heads with discussions on abstruse metaphysical and theological questions, while it would be by far preferable to choose questions from the positive sciences, (*las ciencias de cosas.*) And rhetoric is taught in a foreign language, while the only chance for using it to advantage is in the mother-tongue. Mathematics are almost entirely neglected, to the great disadvantage of the country, and the little that is taught is taught in Latin. There is no professorship of agriculture, architecture, the military sciences; but there are a large number of professorships for vain sophistries; moral philosophy is only taught by name. In medicine anatomy is studied but little, and there is no professorship for materia medica; the case has happened that a physician killed his patient because he mistook *chalybs* for chalk." In civil law people scarcely understood the terms of the law, and the commentators preferred the most barbarous Latin to Spanish. Roman law is of undisputed value, but it would seem a better policy to pay more attention to the law of the Spanish kingdom. The study of theology had entirely degenerated; instead of explaining the patristic writings, the vague and dreamy works of some modern authors were read. "What has become of the analytical method of Aristotle and Euclid?" he exclaims. "Do the students of theology know the Old and the New Testament? Are the future preachers made acquainted with the speeches of the great pulpit orators?" Simon Abril, however, is shrewd enough to add that he was ready to retract anything in his memorial which would not meet with the approval of the Holy Church. It was, indeed, dangerous to speak with so much freedom.

STATE OF EDUCATION DURING THE FIRST HALF OF THE EIGHTEENTH CENTURY.

Philip V. (1701-1746) was much grieved at the mental decadence of his country, which, during the period of the war of the Spanish succession, was a great deal worse than during the time of Simon Abril. Following the example of his grandfather, Louis XIV., he considered it one of the first duties of a king to protect arts and sciences. In 1713 he founded the Royal Academy at Madrid, whose chief duty it was to purify the Castilian language, which, through bad taste and ignorance, had become deteriorated, and in 1738 he established the Academy of History, whose works even now enjoy a well-merited reputation. From his reign there dates the establishment of the Medical Society at Seville, of the Academy of Science at Barcelona, the Academy of History and Geography at Valladolid, and the Academy of Mathematics at Granada. Ferdinand VI. (1746-1759) founded and endowed several universities. A real reform of public instruction, however, was made by Charles III., (1759–1788;) and it was high time, for the wretched condition of affairs at this period beggars description. The text-books and methods of instruction were still the same as in the age of Ximenes; scholasticism ruled supreme, the Copernican system was looked upon with suspicion, and Bacon was not even known by name. The professorship of mathematics at the University of Salamanca had been vacant for one hundred and thirty years, when Diego de Torres was called to fill it. This was the same Torres who, after having studied at Salamanca for five years, with regard to a dissertation of Pedro Clavijo, *De sphæra*, wrote the following words: "I believe this was the first intimation I received that there was such a thing as mathematics." But few Spaniards during the first half of the eighteenth century were enlightened enough not to believe in astrology. When Charles III. requested the University of Salamanca to give up its old prejudices, and to institute lectures on mathematics and natural sciences, the first answer the faculty gave was, "that Newton taught nothing from which logicians and metaphysicians could learn anything, and that the doctrines of Descartes and Gassendi did not agree as well with Divine truth as revealed in the Scriptures as those of Aristotle." In a report made to the king by the minister of state, Marques de Enseñada, we read: "In the whole kingdom there is not a single professorship of law, of natural sciences, of anatomy, and of botany. We have no good map of Spain and its provinces, and no man who could draw such a map, and we are obliged to use the very imperfect maps of Spain which we receive from the Netherlands and from France, so that we, to our great disgrace, do not know the right location and true distance of our own cities."

STATE OF EDUCATION DURING THE SECOND HALF OF THE EIGHTEENTH CENTURY.

The monk Benito Feyoo had had the courage to protest loudly against the prevailing ignorance in his work, *Teatro critico universal ó discursos varios en todo genero de materias, para desengaño de errores comunes*, published in 1726, and he may justly be called the forerunner of all the reforms of Charles III. This king, with the assistance of wise and energetic ministers, boldly laid the ax to the rotten tree. He commenced by limiting the power of the inquisition; he decreed that the authors of works which had been placed on the Index by the Pope, should be permitted to defend themselves publicly before the authorities; that no papal bull should be valid in Spain if not approved by the king; and finally, to crown his work, he banished the Jesuits without consulting the Pope. The universities of Salamanca, Alcala, Granada, and Valencia were reconstructed on an entirely new basis; the monks were directed to apply themselves to study, and various societies for the advancement of education were encouraged and assisted; and in the towns and villages higher and lower schools were opened. Spain felt the beneficial result of the reforms materially and morally; the hopes and expectations which were entertained with regard to the successor of Charles III., Charles IV., (1788-1808,) were, however, not realized. T. Fritz, in his work, *Esquisse d'un cours complet d'éducation et d'instruction*, Strasbourg, 1843, says: "Manuel Godoy, the first minister of Charles IV., declared himself strongly in favor of the Pestalozzian system. A committee appointed to examine the system, after long consultation, finally declared it to be excellent. It had been successfully introduced in the military school at Tarragona, and a school for scholars, established on the same plan in Madrid, continued to prosper in spite of the violent intrigues against it. Zealous teachers who wished to complete their pedagogical studies came to attend this school from all parts of the kingdom, and one of the king's sons was even educated according to the new method. But public opinion was so strong against Godoy, that reforms undertaken by him were not lasting." Documents from the first year of the present century show that the number of schools at that time was still very small; from Easter till the end of October they were closed; the Piarists had the monopoly of public instruction, and private instruction was in the hands of menials. In 1807 a plan of reform was drawn up, in accordance with the system adopted at Salamanca, but it was never carried out.

THE FRENCH INVASION.

The misfortunes of the following years naturally turned all thoughts into another direction. The treachery of Godoy, who betrayed his country to Napoleon I., the abdication of Charles IV., the French invasion, and the accession of Joseph Bonaparte to the throne of Spain, spread the ideas of the French revolution of 1798 throughout Spain, and awakened a strong national sentiment, but the influence of a fanatic priesthood at the same time became stronger and more wide-spread than ever before. The liberals, nevertheless, in the assembly of the Cortes at Cadiz, who drew up a new constitution in 1812, gained a victory over the conservatives. But when Ferdinand VII. returned to Spain, (May 4, 1814,) he refused to take the oath on the new constitution, and was for this loudly applauded by the ignorant masses. The monks and Jesuits reappeared everywhere, the least liberal movement created suspicions in the heart of the despot, and a system of proscriptions commenced, as bad as in the worst times of the monarchy. The welfare of the nation was entirely lost sight of, and civilization was thrown back for a century.

THE CONSTITUTION OF 1812.

From the following articles from the constitution of 1812, it will be seen what progress Spain might have made if it had been carried out loyally by an energetic and enlightened king. Article 366 says: "In all villages of the monarchy primary schools are to be established, in which the children will be taught reading, writing, and arithmetic, the catechism of the Catholic Church, and a summary of the duties of a citizen." Article 367: "A sufficient number of universities and other higher institutions of learning is to be established to teach sciences, literature, and art." Article 368: "The course of instruction is to be uniform in all parts of the kingdom. The constitution is to be taught and explained at all universities and institutions of learning whose course embraces theology and law." Article 369: "A supreme educational committee is to be appointed, consisting of men of acknowledged learning, and the inspection of primary schools is to be in the hands of this committee." Article 370: "The Cortes will, by special laws, regulate all the affairs pertaining to this highly important subject of public instruction." All these articles remained pious wishes. The revolution of 1820 compelled Ferdinand VII. to accept the constitution, the law for a reform of public instruction was made the order of the day, and was published June 29, 1821, but the government did not pay any attention to this. Two years later the civil war broke out, and the attitude taken by the great powers of Europe brought about a complete triumph of the reactionary party.

THE PERIOD OF CIVIL WARS.

A new plan drawn up in opposition to the exertions of the Cortes in 1824 was carried out, and up to the year 1845 no changes were made in it. During the lifetime of Ferdinand VII., education rapidly declined; several universities were deprived of their entire property. The first report of the society for public instruction in Madrid, published in 1839, says: "It is scarcely credible, but nevertheless true, that, *e. g.*, during the reign of the Calomarde ministry in 1827, the sums intended for the salaries of professors of Hebrew and Arabic were appropriated by the government to pay for a school of bull-fighting!" Matters became worse till Christine ascended the throne, (1830;) she reopened the universities, and the royal ordinance of September 29, 1836, had a beneficial influence, increasing the schools and improving their organization. In the year 1838, the Cortés were engaged in discussing two new plans for a reform of public instruction, the first regarding the primary schools, and the other the secondary and superior schools. Only the first plan was adopted, and primary instruction was now regulated by law; the second did not become a law, and the ordinance of 1836 remained in force. It was discussed once more, but bitter party-warfare and civil disturbances for a long time prevented all reforms.

RECENT HISTORY, 1845–1873.

The "plan of studies" of September 17, 1845, promulgated in the beginning of the reign of Isabella II., during the military dictatorship of Narvaez, who had formed a ministry composed entirely of "*moderados*," for the first time embraced the schools of all grades. Normal-schools were established in the chief cities of the provinces; a mining-school and a school of industrial engineering were likewise founded. Narvaez, however, only maintained his position by terrorizing the nation and by the discord among the leaders of the liberal party, and the following eleven years present a deplorable spectacle, as education was suffering greatly through the constant changes of government. The "plan of studies" of 1845, being changed continually, lost its uniformity and finally fell into disuse. In 1851, a concordat with Rome was signed, whose second article says: "Instruction in the universities, colleges, seminaries, public or private schools of every kind, must in all respects be regulated according to the doctrines of the holy Catholic religion. The bishops and clerical superintendents of dioceses are therefore empowered to watch over the purity of morals and the education of youth in all schools, public and private." In the same year the Jesuits again made their appearance in the province of Guipuzcoa; their establishment was closed, however, in 1854, in consequence of the political crisis, which for two years lifted the liberal party into power. Under the influence of the modern Catholic reaction of 1856, on the eve of a change of ministry, the law of September 9, 1857, was promulgated, which in its most essential features has been left unchanged by all the following cabinets, even up to the recent proclamation of the republic. In September, 1868, a revolution broke out by which Queen Isabella was obliged to leave the country. The monks and Jesuits were banished, the concordat with Rome was publicly burned on the 4th of October, 1868, and the constitution of June 9, 1869, made education compulsory and free of charge.

On the 4th of December, 1870, Amadeus, son of King Victor Emanuel of Italy, accepted the crown of Spain, which had been offered to him by the Cortes, but, tired of the never-ending troubles, he abdicated in February, 1873, and the republic was proclaimed in Madrid. Thus an entirely new era has commenced in the history of Spain, and it is difficult to foretell what the end will be and how education will be influenced by these sweeping political changes. The most important points of the law of 1857, and the modifications which have been made in it, are given below.

THE EDUCATIONAL LAW OF 1857.

The law of September 9, 1857, had during a few months been supplanted by the law of June 2, 1868, the work of the most extreme absolutistic and clerical party.

The provisional government of 1868 immediately rescinded this law and returned to the one of 1857, at any rate till something better was created, so as to take education and its supervision out of the hands of the clergy. Don Manuel Ruiz Zorilla, minister of public instruction, in his two decrees of October 4 and 21, 1868, did not conceal his dissatisfaction with the law of 1857. He even went further: in announcing a speedy and thorough reform of the whole system of public instruction, he declared that his ideal was nothing less than the total suppression of all public institutions of learning, as in his opinion this sacrifice was the unavoidable consequence of the constitutional liberty which had been proclaimed. But as during the period of transition the just demands of the moment had to be taken into account, he agreed to a compromise, consisting in the maintenance of the law of 1857, except in such articles as were utterly at variance with the principles of the present government.

SUPREME EDUCATIONAL AUTHORITY.

The highest educational authority is a minister *del fomento*, (of furtherance of education, public works, &c.) According to the law of 1857 the minister was to be assisted in his functions by a "royal council of studies," (*Real consejo de instruccion publica*,) whose president, members, and secretary were to be appointed by the government. This council originally consisted of thirty members, but was reduced to twenty-four by the royal decree of October 9, 1866. There were in this council ministers, archbishops, bishops, councilors of state, directors of public instruction who had formerly been professors in some university, magistrates, state attorneys, members of the royal academies, rectors of universities who had been out of office for six years, ordinary professors of universities, and four places were reserved to men holding no official position, but distinguished by their literary or scientific activity. The office of councilor of studies was entirely honorary, without any emolument whatever, and could never be held by professors in active service. Originally this council had five sections, which by a ministerial decree of June 17, 1868, were reduced to three, viz. one for primary schools, special schools, and schools of art; one for secondary schools; and one for superior schools.

The government was obliged to consult this council with regard to, 1, all changes in the existing laws; 2, the founding or discontinuing of schools of all grades; 3, the founding of new professorships; 4, their salaries and classification, the pensions of teachers, &c.; 5, changes in the course of instruction; 6, choice of text-books; 7, in all other cases provided for by the law and regulations. The minister was also to consult this council on all doubtful questions.

The decree of October 10, 1868, simply abolished this council, and all further measures have been taken under the sole responsibility of the minister. The council had in reality become practically useless, as education had been declared free in the fullest sense of the word, and as the clergy could no longer exercise any influence.

PROVINCIAL AND LOCAL EDUCATIONAL AUTHORITIES.

At the head of the central administration there is a general director of public instruction, while the local administration is in the hands of the rectors of the universities, each of whom is assisted in the exercise of his functions by a local (university) council of education, one for each university district. By royal decree of July 17, 1857, there is to be a provincial council of education in the capital of each province, which is to watch over the progress of education in the primary and secondary schools, and over the proper use of the school fund. According to the law of September 9, 1857, this council was to consist of the governor of the province as president, a member of the provincial diet, a member of the city council, (of the capital of the province,) the school inspector of the province, a clergyman, proposed by the bishop of the province, and at least two private citizens, fathers of families. Finally there was to be a local (district) council of education in every district of the province, for the supervision of primary instruction, consisting of the alcalde, one district councilor, one clergyman of the district, and at least two fathers of families. This local (district) council had to report to the provincial council, and this to the rector of the university, who again reported to the central government. All these regulations were changed by the decree of October 14, 1868; henceforth the provincial councils are to consist of nine members elected by the provincial diets; the local (district) councils are to consist of fifteen members in cities of more than 100,000 inhabitants, in cities of fewer inhabitants, not less than 2,000, of nine members; in all others of five members, who are to be elected by the city councils. All these measures clearly show the prevailing spirit of decentralization, while from 1845 till the revolution of 1868 the opposite principle had ruled almost exclusively.

PRIMARY INSTRUCTION.

Primary instruction is divided into two grades, elementary and higher. The course of instruction in the elementary grade comprises the following subjects: Christian doctrine and sacred history, reading, writing, principles of Spanish grammar, orthography, principles of arithmetic, with the legal system of weights, measures, and coins, rudiments of agriculture, industry, and commerce, adapted to the localities. The higher primary grade is to embrace in addition the following subjects: principles of geometry, linear drawing and surveying, rudiments of history and geography, especially of Spain, general notions of natural philosophy and natural history as adapted to the necessities of every-day life. In the girls' schools female work and domestic hygiene are substituted for the rudiments of agriculture, industry, and commerce.

STATISTICS.

There are no later statistics of primary instruction than those of 1867, but for comparison's sake those of 1797 and 1859 are also given:
Number of public and private primary schools in 1797, 11,156.
Number of public and private primary schools in 1859, 22,060.

Number of public and private primary schools in 1867, 26,332.

Number of scholars in public and private primary schools in 1797, 400,376.

Number of scholars in public and private primary schools in 1859, 1,086,578.

Number of scholars in public and private primary schools in 1867, 1,425,339.

SECONDARY INSTRUCTION.

The so-called secondary schools for a long time taught nothing but a little Latin and moral philosophy, but other branches of instruction have now been introduced, such as modern languages, geography, history, mathematics, logic, chemistry, natural philosophy, gymnastics, fencing, music, &c. These schools are called *Institutos*. They are maintained chiefly by provincial and local exertion. According to the statistics of 1867 there were 63 secondary schools, viz, 50 provincial and 13 local, with 18,903 scholars.

NORMAL SCHOOLS.

The law of 1857 created primary normal-schools in the capital of every province, besides a central normal-school at Madrid. The latter is supported by the central government, and the others by the provincial authorities. With each of these normal-schools a model- or practice-school is connected. The course of studies is two years for teachers of the lower primary grade, three years for those of the higher primary grade, and four years for the diploma of *maestro de escuela normal*. The course of instruction in the central normal-school embraces the following subjects: Universal history, history of Spain, rhetoric, poetry, geography, grammar, pedagogics with special reference to the instruction of the blind and the deaf and dumb, natural philosophy, chemistry, natural history, industry, commerce, systems and methods of instruction, geometry, linear drawing, agriculture, religion and morals, theory and practice of reading and writing, gymnastics. The course of instruction in the provincial normal-schools is very similar.

SUPERIOR INSTRUCTION.

Superior instruction comprises the "Faculties," (the universities,) and some special schools, which will be mentioned below. There are at present ten universities, which number is justly considered too large. These ten universities, which at the same time are the seats of the local (university) councils, are Madrid, (embracing the provinces of Madrid, Ciudad Real, Cuenca, Guadalajara, Segovia, and Toledo;) Barcelona, (Barcelona, Gerona, Lerida, Taragona, and the Balearic Islands;) Granada, (Granada, Almeria, Jaen, and Malaga;) Oviedo, (Oviedo and Leon;) Salamanca, (Salamanca, Avila, Caceres, and Zamora;) Santiago,

(Coruña, Lugo, Orense, and Pontevedra;) Seville, (Seville, Badajoz, Cadiz, Canary Islands, Cordova, Huelva;) Valencia, (Valencia, Albacete, Alicante, Castellon, Murcia;) Valladolid, (Valladolid, Alava, Burgos, Guipuzcoa, Viscaya;) Saragossa, (Saragossa, Huesca, Logroño, Navarra, Soria, Teruel.)

Every university has a rector, appointed by the government from among the professors, (decree of October 14, 1868.) There is also a vice-rector, one of the professors, who takes the rector's place in case of absence or sickness. The reform produced by the revolution of 1868 has not had much influence on the universities. All that has been done was to revise the lecture-plan, to suppress the theological faculty, and to empower all universities to give the doctor degree, which privilege had been confined to the University of Madrid. There are three academical degrees: Baccalaureate, licentiate, and doctor. Each university is to have five faculties, viz: 1. Philosophy and Literature; 2. Mathematical and Natural Sciences; 3. Pharmacy; 4. Medicine; 5. Law. Not all universities, however, possess all these five faculties. In the University of Madrid they are all represented. With the second faculty in Madrid there is connected a school of mathematics, physics, and chemistry, a museum of natural history, and an astronomical observatory. Law faculties are at present found in all universities. Faculties of medicine are only in Madrid, Granada, Santiago, Seville, Valencia, and Valladolid; and faculties of pharmacy are only found in Madrid, Barcelona, and Granada.

SPECIAL INSTRUCTION.

Of special schools Spain possesses the following: 1. The special schools for engineers and miners at Madrid; 2. The schools of agriculture at Madrid and Aranjuez; 3. The industrial schools at Madrid and Barcelona; 4. The *escuela diplomatica* (school of diplomacy) at Madrid; 5. The lower law-schools (for educating public notaries) at Madrid, Barcelona, Granada, Oviedo, and Valladolid; 6. The academy of the fine arts at Madrid, the school of architecture at Madrid, the conservatory of music at Madrid; 7. The schools of veterinary surgery at Madrid, (of the first class,) and those of the second class at Cordova, Leon, and Saragossa; 8. The navigation schools at Barcelona, Bilbao, Cadiz, Cartagena, Coruña, Gijon, Malaga, San Sebastian, Santander, and Santa Cruz, (on the island of Teneriffe;) and the schools of ship-building at Barcelona, Cadiz, Coruña, and Santander.

EDUCATION IN BOLIVIA.

EDUCATION IN BOLIVIA.

[NOTE.—For the following account of education in Bolivia we are indebted to the report of the Brazilian minister in La Paz, Bolivia, made to the Brazilian government in April, 1872, and kindly forwarded to this Bureau by the Brazilian minister at Washington.]

CONSTITUTIONAL PROVISIONS REGARDING EDUCATION.

The constitution of Bolivia guarantees liberty of instruction under the supervision of the state; but this principle, although acknowledged by the constitution of 1851, has never been carried into practical execution as far as superior and professional instruction is concerned, and only to a certain limited extent with regard to primary and secondary instruction. The ministry of public instruction has, on different occasions, denied the authority for liberty of instruction in professional studies, thus openly defying the letter of the constitution. This difference dates from the university statute of November 13, 1846, dictated under the influence of the political constitution of 1843.

HISTORY OF PUBLIC INSTRUCTION.

The history of public instruction in Bolivia presents no very flattering picture. During the colonial period primary schools supported by the government were almost entirely unknown. Only in the beginning of this century primary schools were founded in some cities under the supervision of, and supported by, the respective city councils. Primary instruction was consequently confined to some private schools of the most imperfect description, and to the convent-schools; as a general rule, reading and writing were taught in the parental home. Superior instruction was limited to Latin and the outline of philosophy taught at the University of Saint Francis Xavier, established in Charcas almost at the same time when the Jesuits founded seminaries at Chuquisaca and La Paz, during the reign of Charles III., (1759–1788.) The University of Charcas was one of the most noted of the few high-schools that promoted civilization on the South American continent. Besides the above-mentioned studies, ecclesiastical and civil law were taught, and many men who distinguished themselves during the struggle for independence, such as Monteagudo and Moreno, studied at this university. The professors were men of acknowledged ability, and many of their scholars, especially among the law students, gained a great reputation, such as Pinto and Origüela. The splendor of the University of Charcas disappeared with the declaration of independence. General Sucre (first president of Bolivia, 1825–1828) organized several colleges for secondary instruction in the principal cities, and promised the establishment of primary schools in the provinces, a few of which were really established. In 1831 another university was founded in La Paz, introducing a more extended amount of preparatory studies. Although not yet sufficient, law, medicine, and theology are included. In 1846 another change took place in the system of public instruction. In that year, Frias, minister of public instruction, promulgated a new educational statute, by which instruction of all kinds was divided in three grades, viz, primary, secondary, and professional, and with regard to the two last-mentioned introduced, though in a very imperfect manner, the French system of simultaneous instruction. The adoption of this system was, in Bolivia, considered a progress, and although many now deplore the numerous imperfections of this system, it is still followed with but few alterations. One of the chief faults of the system of secondary instruction is, that too much time is devoted to mere literary or humanitarian studies, thus neglecting the more scientific studies. Thus the study of chemistry, natural philosophy, and natural history is limited to a mere nomenclature of aphorisms; and the want of special schools only increases this evil. Another great complaint raised against the present system is the want of professors, whose number is so limited that most of them have to teach a great number of frequently very heterogeneous subjects. In the year 1859, Valle, the minister of public instruction, promulgated new statutes of public instruction (extending also to the primary schools) fashioned after the French system, thus producing a veritable chaos in educational affairs. From this rapid review it will be seen that education in Bolivia leaves still much to be desired.

PRIMARY INSTRUCTION.

Primary instruction is given in city- and cantonal-schools, (canton: subdivision of the province, answering to our counties,) infant-schools, (*casas de asylo,*) and female colleges, (*collegios de educandas.*) The course of instruction in the city-schools embraces Christian doctrine, reading, writing, arithmetic, Spanish geography and history; and in the cantonal schools, Christian doctrine, writing, reading, elements of arithmetic, and Spanish. The number of city- and cantonal schools are proportioned to the number of inhabitants. The teachers are appointed and paid by the government, whose duty it is to increase the number of schools wherever it is deemed necessary. In order to educate competent primary teachers there is to be established a normal-school in the capital of every department, (province.) All schools are regulated by the law of November 13, 1846, and by the law of December 31, 1859. In addition, the following educational laws are in force: The law of

April 20, 1860, treating of the expenses for gratuitous instruction and of the conduct of the examinations; the law of August 25, 1860, treating of the competitive courses for teachers and of the number of scholars in each school; the law of December 7, 1860, treating of the appointment of teachers; and the law of July 7, 1862, regulating the school at Cochabamba, conducted by the Sisters of Charity. The law of June 27, 1861, whose execution is recommended by the order of July 20, 1864, provides in its 8th paragraph: "In villages where there is no state-school, the priests will, at their own expense, keep a school in which the elements of religion are taught and primary instruction is given." By decree of November 25, 1867, central schools of primary instruction have been established in the capitals of some of the departments. By a circular of September 3, 1856, primary-school committees are appointed in the capitals of the departments, having the duty to supervise the schools of their departments, to establish new schools where it is found necessary, and to improve the existing schools. By a decree of December 10, 1859, the art-colleges of La Paz and Cochabamba are converted into schools for the children of workingmen. By a decree of September, 1861, the primary schools are divided into complete and incomplete schools.

INFANT-SCHOOLS.

The first infant-school was established on November 23, 1855, in the city of Potosi, intended to prepare young children between the ages of three and seven years for the primary schools. July 20, 1858, another was established at Sucre, and finally, August 20, 1861, a third one at Cochabamba; this is the one to which the law of July 2, 1862, refers, intrusting it to the care of the Sisters of Charity, and assigning to it a house and funds.

FEMALE COLLEGES.

There are female colleges (*collegios de educandas*) in the capital cities of the departments. The course of instruction in these institutions embraces reading, writing, arithmetic, Christian doctrine, Spanish grammar, universal history, Old and New Testament, geometry, cosmography, natural philosophy, physical geography, domestic hygiene, drawing, music, embroidery, cutting, and sewing. These colleges are under the immediate direction of a lady principal, and are subject to the inspection of a committee composed of one member of the university-council, a magistrate, and a clergyman, presided over by the vice-chancellor of the university. These colleges admit both day-scholars and boarders, some of whom receive instruction free of charge, whose number is fixed by the law of January 18, 1862. On November 23 such a college was established at Santa Cruz; in 1863 the second at Oruro; in 1864 the third at Tarija, and in 1866 the college at La Paz was transformed into a day-school.

SECONDARY INSTRUCTION.

Secondary instruction is imparted in secular and ecclesiastical colleges. The course of instruction in the former, which are government institutions, embraces languages, arithmetic, algebra, geometry, trigonometry, geography, history, elements of natural history, natural philosophy, religion and moral philosophy, drawing, and vocal and instrumental music, (decree of October 15, 1845.) Each college has six classes, and the professors are appointed by the government after a competitive examination. Most of the capitals of departments possess such colleges, admitting also day scholars. The ecclesiastical colleges or seminaries (*collegios seminarios*) are under the direction of the clerical authorities, and are regulated by special laws. Their course is very similar to that of the secular colleges, only giving more extensive instruction in theology. Nothing, however, must be taught that is contrary to the constitution or the laws of the country. By a decree of February 25, 1859, the archbishop of Charcas established grand or central ecclesiastical seminaries in the dioceses of La Paz, Cochabamba, and Santa Cruz, under the direction of the respective prelates. Bolivia also possesses some private lyceums or secondary schools, established under a license from the government.

SUPERIOR INSTRUCTION.

Bolivia has three universities, viz, Sucre, La Paz, and Cochabamba. The direction and inspection of schools of every grade are entirely in the hands of the universities. Each university has five faculties, viz: 1. Theology; 2. Law and political sciences; 3. Medicine; 4. Mathematical and physical sciences; 5. Humanities and philosophy. The faculty of theology comprises dogmatics, morals, ecclesiastical law, sacred history, and church history, (decree of November 24, 1840.) The faculty of law comprises civil law of Bolivia, Roman law, as applied in Bolivia, elements of political economy, commercial law, judicial organization, criminal law, medical jurisprudence, constitutional law, and administrative law, (decrees of November 27 and December 27, 1859, and June 5, 1864.) The faculty of medicine comprises anatomy, physiology, pathology, materia medica, chemistry, pharmacy, hygiene, and clinical practice. The faculty of mathematical and physical sciences comprises mathematics, natural history, chemistry, and natural philosophy. The faculty of humanities and philosophy comprises literature, philosophy, and history. The degrees conferred by the universities are, bachelor, licentiate, and doctor; the medical faculty only confers the degree of doctor. All instruction at the universities must have for its basis: 1, the precepts of the holy Catholic religion; 2, fidelity to the republic, to the constitution, and the principles of public order; 3, obedience to the statutes of the university. The officers of the university are: 1, the minister of public instruction, (the highest authority;) 2, the chancellor; 3, the vice-chancellor; 4, the councilors; 5, the ordinary councilors; 6, the deans and professors of faculties; 7, the presidents and professors of colleges; 8, the directors and professors of private institutions of learning licensed by the university. The university-council is composed of ten members, two of whom are inspecting councilors, and one chosen from among the presidents of colleges appointed for lifetime, (*conselheros perpetuos;*) the seven others are ordinary councilors, chosen from among the deans and professors of faculties, and from among the presidents and professors of colleges. The minister appoints these seven ordinary councilors every year. In order to become "perpetual councilor," a person must have been employed ten years at some college, and have served five years in the council as ordinary councilor.

ACADEMIES OF FORENSIC PRACTICE.

These academies were created by a decree of April 23, 1859, as institutions entirely separate from the universities, with which they had been connected by a decree of November 15, 1855. They are attended by law-students, after having obtained the degree of licentiate, for two or more years, till they are able to present themselves for an examination for attorney before the district courts. These academies are under the immediate supervision of a committee composed of several judicial authorities and lawyers of the district.

ART-COLLEGES.

By a decree of August 6, 1853, two such colleges were established in the republic, and by a decree of the 25th August, of the same year, instruction in these colleges was declared entirely free of charge. The course of instruction is not given, but these colleges are a sort of industrial or technical schools.

MINING-SCHOOLS.

By a decree of August 6, 1853, mining-schools were founded in the cities of Potosi and Oruro.

LIBRARIES AND PUBLIC MUSEUMS.

Public libraries were established by a decree of June 30, 1858, and by a decree of March 14, 1867, special libraries were established at the universities and the institutions of secondary instruction. All the public libraries are under the direction and supervision of the university-councils, and there is a director-in-chief of all the public libraries of the republic. By a decree of December 31, 1840, public museums were established in the capitals of every province. The most important of these museums are those of Potosi, founded in 1846, and of La Paz, founded in 1845.

AGRICULTURAL COLLEGE.

By a law of June 12, 1861, an agricultural college was to be established, which was opened on the 26th October, in Cochabamba. By a decree of August 3, 1864, this college was, however, abolished, and the law of September, 1865, decreed that a general knowledge of agriculture should be imparted in the primary schools.

EDUCATION IN URUGUAY.

EDUCATION IN URUGUAY.

[NOTE.—For the following account of education in Uruguay we are indebted to the report of the Brazilian minister in Montevideo, made to the Brazilian government in March, 1872, and kindly forwarded to this Bureau by the Brazilian minister at Washington.]

LEGAL PROVISIONS FOR PUBLIC INSTRUCTION.

As far back as May 16, 1827, the government of Uruguay, with laudable zeal, established public elementary schools, recognizing them as one of the first necessities of free nations. According to a decree published on the above-mentioned date, a primary school, on the Lancasterian plan, was to be founded at the expense of the national treasury in every town, with a teacher employed at a salary of sixty pesos per month; every child aged seven years or upward should be admitted to these schools free of charge. In every place where a school had been established, there was to be an inspecting committee, composed of a judge and two citizens. This committee was to inspect the schools, to watch the conduct of the teacher and the affairs of the school, and finally to make a report to the government.

On September 13, 1847, a decree was passed creating a new educational authority, to which the management and supervision of primary instruction was intrusted. The preamble of this decree deserves to be given entire: " Education is the creative germ of the happiness and prosperity of nations, because in it dwells the knowledge which produces good institutions, and public and private virtue. The study of its development, its application, and its tendency is not the work of speculation, of individual belief, or of sectarian interests, but belongs exclusively to the government. Being the sole executive of the people whom it represents, to it alone should be confided the sacred trust of the dogmas and principles which form the basis of the very existence of society; on it alone rests the responsibility, and it is its undeniable duty to take possession of the feelings, ideas, and instincts of man from his birth, and to mold them so as to fit him for the conditions and exigencies of the society in which he is to live. In no other way can a commonwealth exist, or can there be that social harmony without which a state possesses neither order and tranquillity nor strength and life. In view of all this the government has decided to devote all its energies to this subject, and has for the safety of the republic decreed," &c.

The duties of this authority, or educational council, are: 1, to promote, diffuse, make uniform and systematize public and, more especially, primary instruction; 2, to authorize or forbid the opening of every kind of educational institution; 3, to regulate the conditions on which it is to exist; 4, to examine the works and doctrines which are to form the basis of the study of moral sciences; 5, to inspect all educational institutions and to correct abuses; 6, to watch studiously over the observance of the most perfect harmony between education and the political and religious beliefs which form the basis of the social fabric; 7, to propose to the government improvements in public instruction. The number of the members of this council was fixed at twelve, to be appointed by the government, with the minister of the interior as president. Vacancies in the council are to be filled through election by the members, the vote being approved by the government. All expenses connected with this council are to be paid from the national treasury.

By decree of March 13, 1848, the regulations for primary schools, public and private, proposed by this council, were sanctioned by the government. Primary instruction was divided into two grades, a lower and a higher one, those schools being termed "complete schools" which embraced both grades. The course of instruction in the "lower primary schools" embraces the following subjects: 1, Christian doctrine and principles of morality; 2, reading; 3, writing; 4, the four fundamental rules of arithmetic; 5, Spanish grammar; 6, outlines of the geography of Uruguay. The course of instruction in the "higher primary schools" embraces: 1, the same studies as in the lower primary schools, only carried further; besides: 2, some knowledge of the privileges and duties of citizens; 3, linear drawing and elements of geometry; 4, cosmography and general geography; 5, outlines of the history of Uruguay and its constitution.

All public schools should, if possible, contain two grades of primary instruction, and be divided into two sections. Pupils who have finished their studies in the upper section ought to be fully capable of entering some institution of secondary instruction.

The teachers in the public schools are appointed by the educational council from among a number of competitors. To obtain a place as teacher in primary schools, both lower and higher, it is necessary, 1, to be not less than eighteen years of age; 2, to produce a certificate of good moral character; 3, to pass a competitive examination. When all these conditions have been fulfilled the "council" issues a teacher's certificate. Teachers enjoy the following privileges: 1, exemption from military service; 2, exemption from any and all municipal offices; 3, exemption from any public service not connected with education. The following persons can never hold the office of teacher: 1, those who at any time have been condemned to a defamatory punishment; 2, those who are under the accusation of any crime; 3, those who have been declared guilty of fraudulent bankruptcy.

Private schools may be established in any part of the republic, but their programme and course of instruction must previously have been submitted to the "educational council" for approbation, with the sole object that it may contain nothing against public morals or the constitution of the country. Pupils from private schools may be admitted to public schools after rendering proof, by an examination, of their having studied all the subjects prescribed in the public schools. No private school can have more than eight pupils; as soon as this number is exceeded it is considered a public school, and is subject to the same regulations as the public schools.

In no educational institution, either public or private, can any other punishments be inflicted except the following: 1, repetition of the lessons; 2, increased lessons; 3, keeping in after school-hours; 4, standing during school-hours; 5, public notification of expulsion; 6, private or public expulsion. The last-mentioned punishment can only be inflicted for very grave offenses, and only after three notifications.

Teachers who are derelict in their duties are warned, then punished by fines, and finally suspended.

In order to carry out these regulations the council appoints every three months a committee of two from among its members to inspect every school as often as is convenient, but not less than once a month.

The schools in the other departments of the republic (outside of the department of Montevideo) are managed by the respective municipal corporations, under the direction of the "educational council."

The inspecting committee must, at the end of every quarter, make a report to the "educational council" on the general state of the schools, the number of pupils, &c.

Girls' schools are subject to the same laws and regulations as boys' schools, only that more regard is taken to the wants of females by teaching sewing and other female work.

Such is the legislation regarding primary instruction in Uruguay, which, during the twenty-five years it has been in force, would have produced the most beneficial results but for the constant political disturbances, which have prevented the proper carrying-out of many provisions of the educational law, and have kept especially the rural population in a state of deplorable ignorance.

STATISTICS.

The most recent statistics are those of 1868; only of the capital, Montevideo, and the department of that name, there are statistics of the year 1871.

Educational Statistics of 1868.

DEPARTMENTS.	SCHOOLS.			SCHOLARS.		
	For boys.	For girls.	Total.	Boys.	Girls.	Total.
Montevideo:						
Free-schools supported by the municipality of the department	24	20	44	2,269	2,265	4,534
Schools supported by a philanthropical association			2			240
Private schools licensed by the government	13	12	25	1,372	667	2,039
Children educated in schools having no government license or at home						1,200
Total of Montevideo, city and department			71			8,013
Canelones			13			598
Salto			11			642
Paysandú			8			476
Cerro Largo			7			488
Colonia			6			344
Soriano			6			330
Tacuarambó			6			307
Maldonado			6			403
José			5			347
Florida			8			216
Minas			4			310
Carmelo			3			296
Durazno			3			248
Total			86			5,005
Total of the whole republic			157			13,018

In the year 1871 the number of scholars in the public schools of the department of Montevideo had considerably diminished, being only 4,995, viz, 2,021 boys and 2,974 girls. The number of pupils in private schools licensed by the government has increased, as in 1871 it was 2,430, viz, 1,714 boys and 716 girls. The number of children receiving instruction in schools having no government license or at home was, in 1871, 3,680, showing a remarkable increase. To appreciate these figures, we give the population of Uruguay according to the *Almanach de Gotha* for 1873: 350,000, and the population of Montevideo about 50,000; including the department, 120,000.

– EDUCATION IN PORTUGAL

EDUCATION IN PORTUGAL.

[NOTE.—The following outline of the educational history of Portugal is taken from an article by Alphons Le Roy, professor in Liège, in the 6th volume of Schmid's *Educational Cyclopedia*.]

EARLY HISTORY.

Portugal is not separated from Spain by any natural boundaries, but from the days of Viriathus and Sertorius it has been independent from that country by the decided wish of the population, who always were firmly attached to their national independence. The Romans, the Goths, and Moors in turn imposed their foreign yoke on the descendants of the old Lusitanians; the first-mentioned left to them the system of regularly organized municipalities, the Goths laid the foundation of the legislative assemblies, in later times called cortes; but neither the former nor the latter were able to change the original type of the inhabitants, or to produce an amalgamation with their neighbors. The Lusitanians were the first nation on the peninsula who conquered the Moors, and for a long time shared the glory of the Spanish chivalry. They did not, however, identify their interests with those of their neighbors; but as soon as possible, in the beginning of the twelfth century, constituted themselves a separate kingdom under a French family of sovereigns. Henry of Burgundy, descendant of Hugh Capet, who had come to the peninsula in search of adventures, and who had married Theresa, the natural daughter of Alphons VI., King of Leon and Castile, was, in the year 1095, by him appointed "Count of Portugal." The name "Portugal," which then appeared for the first time in history, only meant a portion of the province of Beira. After the death of his father-in-law, Henry emancipated himself from the sovereignty of Castile, and his son and successor, Alphons I. Henriquez, definitely adopted the royal title in the year 1140, acknowledging the Pope as his only supreme authority, which protected him against the Castilian claims. During the following century Portugal assumed its present dimensions.

PORTUGAL UNDER THE BURGUNDIAN DYNASTY.

The Burgundian dynasty, which by its foreign policy maintained the honor of Portugal, did no less for the internal development of the country. Portugal, which afterward, through clerical oppression, became a prey to deepest ignorance, was, during the latter half of the thirteenth century, justly considered one of the most enlightened countries of Europe. This it owed chiefly to the excellent prince Dom Diniz, (Dionysius,) called "*o rei lavardor*"—the farmer king—of whom the people, even in our days, sing:

> "O rei Dom Diniz,
> Que fiz quanto quiz!"

i. e., "King Dom Diniz did what he pleased." Educated by a learned French prelate, Aymeric d'Ébrard, who understood how to bring out all the noble qualities of his mind, he did not content himself with the promotion of agriculture and the endeavor to secure the future wealth of his country by founding a navy and extending commerce, but he also sought, as far as lay in his power, to diffuse knowledge among his people. In the year 1290 he founded at Lisbon that famous university which, eighteen years later, was transferred to Coimbra, brought back to Lisbon in 1338 by Alphons II., and finally, in the year 1557, was again firmly established at Coimbra by João III. Dom Diniz did even more; he took (a very rare case in those times) the most active interest in the education of the lower classes by founding elementary schools, which, in his own words, were to enlighten the masses and free them from the superstitions with which the clergy filled their minds, in order more firmly to establish their supremacy. His successors, however, did not follow up this liberal spirit. King Dom Duarte, and his son Alphons V., who founded the first royal library in Portugal, exercised a very beneficial influence on education and science. Alphons especially endeavored to keep step with the development of the Paris University, but the masses did not reap much benefit from King Dom Diniz's noble intentions. Municipal documents from the year 1385 show that in Lisbon the most outrageous superstitions were widely spread, so much so that even the clerical authorities had to use energetic measures for suppressing abuses. There are no official documents whatever regarding elementary education till the eighteenth century. The only fact that can be ascertained has been communicated by Ferdinand Denis, viz, that in 1551 there were in Lisbon 7 teachers of grammar, 34 teachers of reading, 13 public schools for organ-playing, 14 dancing-schools, and four fencing-schools. There were only 2 female teachers who instructed girls in reading! but there were 12 public "letter-writers," and 430 jewelers. This brief statistical notice shows at one glance the whole civilization of Portugal at that period. A Venetian embassador writes, at the end of the sixteenth century, that in Lisbon a large number of Portuguese, Spanish, Italian, and Latin books were for sale, but that the prices were so high that poor students would rather loan the books day by day, paying a certain small sum. The chief school was the school of Santa Cruz, which is praised by all the old historians, and for which several excellent teachers had been especially called from Paris. The University of Coimbra was in the most flourishing condition at the time when Camoens studied there, (1539.) One of the professors, Diego de Gorea, who brought Buchanan to Coimbra, and who defended the philosophy of Aristotle against Ramus, was considered one of the most learned humanists in Europe; Vinceuz Fabricius, a German, taught Greek so thoroughly that Kleynærts (Clenardus) is enthusiastic in his praise; Pedro Nuñez was a famous teacher of mathematics and physics; Brissot, a Frenchman, was a most enlightened professor of medicine, and all the faculties could boast of excellent teachers, who spread the riches of their learning among the eager youth and shone as models of brilliant dialectics.

PORTUGAL UNDER THE AVIZ DYNASTY, 1385-1580.

The royal line of Aviz, which followed the house of Burgundy on the throne of Portugal, devoted its attention chiefly to foreign conquests and discoveries and to the strengthening of the colonial empire. They could not better employ the good natural talents of the Portuguese nation and that chivalrous character which is innate in it. The ocean opened to them a wide field for adventures and invited them to voyages into distant countries. During this glorious period Vasco de Gama (1498) discovered the way to India round the Cape of Good Hope; Francisco de Almeida and Alfonso de Albuquerque founded powerful empires in India; Alvarez Cabral, in 1500, discovered Brazil, and the wealth and power of Portugal reached its zenith. But this countless wealth became the source of decadence, the nation became enervated, emigration depopulated the country, and the sinister activity of the inquisition completed the work of mental and moral decline.

PORTUGAL UNDER SPANISH RULE, 1581-1640.

Religious fanaticism, the most arbitrary despotism, and the greatest disorder in the administration, characterized the period of the Spanish rule; the navy was destroyed, and the rich Indian possessions passed into the hands of the Dutch. The tyranny and avarice of Olivarez, the all-powerful minister of the imbecile Spanish king, Philip IV., at last stirred up the Portuguese people; they revolted in 1640, gained their independence, and intrusted the guidance of their country to the family of Braganza, which is still ruling. Peace with Spain was concluded in 1688, the African possessions and Brazil were returned to Portugal, but the great mass of the people, lulled into a mental sleep by ignorance and superstition, seemed to have forgotten their glorious past. Commerce did not again revive, manufactures passed into the hands of the English, and agriculture was entirely neglected. The Jesuits and the nobility divided the revenue of the country between them. Before proceeding further, it will be necessary to glance back and relate the introduction of the famous Society of Jesus into Portugal.

FIRST ESTABLISHMENT OF THE JESUITS IN PORTUGAL.

In the year 1540 King Dom João IV. asked the papal see to send him two Jesuit fathers, which request was eagerly complied with. One of these was Francis Xavier, the apostle of India. After he, in the following year, had sailed for India, the king immediately determined to found at Coimbra, by the side of the university, that famous Jesuit college from which so many missionaries have gone forth, and which gained such a high reputation in the philosophical world by its faithful adherence to the Aristotelian system of the Middle-Ages. The college at Coimbra was the first the Jesuits possessed in Portugal, and it has always remained their most important stronghold in that country. The so-called "free arts" were taught in this college, *i. e.*, languages, Greek and Hebrew included, belles-lettres and philosophy, corresponding to the lower course of the university; the higher course embracing law, medicine, and theology. The Jesuits obtained from the king the same privileges as the university, and claimed entire independence from that institution. The university, at first indifferent, at last became aroused, and in 1545 forced the college to open its gates and to submit to university inspection. The consequence was a protracted quarrel, which ended in favor of the Jesuits. The nation protested, but in vain; the king personally introduced the Jesuits into a new and liberally endowed building in 1550, for which he himself had drawn the plans. In 1553 the Jesuits were made independent from the university also with regard to theological studies; two years later half the university was in their hands, and all the lay professors were dismissed with life-pensions. A royal ordinance, confirmed by a papal bull, gave to them the whole lower course, established a separate income for them, and freed them from all supervision. In 1558 they obtained the academical privileges for the philosophical examinations, although the university should continue to bear the expense. Since then, in spite of a last desperate effort, education passed entirely into their hands. The College of Coimbra usually numbered 2,000 students, and triumphantly opposed to the advance of modern ideas its philosophical catechism, until the moment when a royal committee, appointed by the energetic minister Pombal, awakened the old complaints against the order, and in judicial form preferred accusations against it.

THE REFORMS OF MINISTER POMBAL.

It would be unjust to trace the whole cause of the downfall of the Portuguese power to the Jesuits, but it must be confessed that they were by no means listless spectators, and that they certainly have not a little contributed toward it. If the annals of their transatlantic missions show many a glorious page, they cannot be declared free of the reproach of having reduced princes and nations in the south of Europe to that state of infancy which was their ideal in Paraguay; they formed a state within the state, and their mysterious power showed itself during two centuries in measures which, in the long run, would have reduced to stupidity the most intelligent nation. Some acts of the great reformer Pombal (Sebastião de Carvalho) may be severely censured, but it will always remain his glory boldly to have cut the Gordian knot. Endowed with an iron will, and with the clearness of a lofty mind, he undertook the grand work of regenerating his country. His burning zeal embraced all the public interests, the army, the navy, agriculture, and, above all, education. He commenced by banishing the Jesuits from the country, and by confiscating all their property. But like Joseph II. of Austria, "he took the second step before the first," and attempted to carry out his reforms by despotic measures. Fallen into disgrace, he died in solitude. Yet his ideas did not die with him. Even in our days does Pombal's spirit animate all the intelligent minds of the Portuguese nation. The order of the Jesuits had thus, by a single stroke of the pen, been banished from its twenty-four great colleges, and had by one blow lost all its influence and wealth. At the same time (July 28, 1759,) the secularization of public instruction was decreed, and faculties of philosophy and mathematics were founded at the University of Coimbra. In the year 1772 Pombal decreed that a primary school should be established in every community in the kingdom; up to that time the number of primary schools in the whole monarchy had not exceeded four hundred. Greek and Latin had hitherto only been taught in the convents; but Pombal established 257 elementary Latin schools, 21 professorships of rhetoric, history, and literature, 27 schools of philosophy, where logic, metaphysics, and moral philosophy were taught in a one-year's course, and finally, 8 Greek schools. Pombal crowned his work by appointing a "superior council of studies," consisting of the rector and five professors of the University of Coimbra, a secretary, and six other officers; he imposed a tax on wine and liquor, which, under the name of "*subsidio literario*," formed the beginning of a regular income for public instruction, and for defraying the expenses of the council of studies, to which the management of all educational institutions throughout the kingdom was intrusted. The theological seminaries, which had been placed under the supervision of the bishops, were endowed with some of the confiscated property; any one, either layman or clergyman, was empowered to open private schools, on the condition of placing them under government inspection and supervision. The University of Coimbra was remodeled according to the plan of Italian universities, and several professors were called from Italy; but the downfall of Pombal, in the year 1777, brought back everything to its former condition.

FROM POMBAL'S DOWNFALL TO THE PRESENT TIME.

After the downfall of Pombal, the ignorant clergy and the narrow-minded and unpatriotic nobility again took the management of the government into their hands. Academical instruction became a common laughing-stock, and there was a time when any one could obtain a degree by sending a servant with the required fees to the respective authorities. The attendance at the elementary schools decreased to such a degree that the average number of scholars dwindled down, from 24,000 in 1807, to 8,000 in 1828.

On account of the mental condition of Queen Maria, widow of Pedro III., who died in 1786, the government was intrusted to the heir to the crown, João VI., the prince of Brazil, in 1799. Wavering between French and English influence, the regent excited the anger of Napoleon I. by his refusal to close his ports to the English. In 1807 Marshal Junot entered Portugal with a French army, and the royal family had to seek refuge in Brazil, where they remained till 1821. The Portuguese complained, and not without cause, that, even after the French had been driven out of the country, they had to be governed from a distant colony, while at the same time Brazil ceased to be treated as a province. The revolution of 1820, which decided the return of the king to Europe, had the immediate consequence of introducing a constitutional government in Portugal; but, as the Portuguese Cortes denied the Brazilians equal rights, they protested and separated from the mother-country, retaining however the Braganza dynasty. The first absolutistic reaction of Dom Miguel proved a failure: his brother, Dom Pedro, the oldest son of Dom João VI., resigned his European crown in favor of his oldest daughter Dona Maria da Gloria. His is the honor of having given to Portugal during his short reign the constitution of April 29, 1826, which, in all its essential points, is still in force. During the following years Portugal had to suffer the tyranny of Dom Miguel, regent till Dona Maria came of age. This state of affairs came to an end in 1832. Two years later Dom Miguel surrendered, Dom Pedro died, and his daughter Dona Maria, declared of age by the Cortes, would have inaugurated a new era of prosperity for her unfortunate country had not the envy and passion of the statesmen, their egotism and ambition on the one hand, and the excited condition of the democratic party on the other, continually produced new disturbances. During the fifteen years 1836–1851 there were no less than seventeen revolutions in Portugal. After the military revolution of Marshal Saldanha in 1851, some changes in the constitution became necessary; the party of progress, which hitherto had known no bounds in opposing the government in the Cortes, now consented to support the government, and lasting peace could be hoped for. The reign of Dom Pedro V. in 1855 commenced under the most favorable auspices, but the young and beloved prince died prematurely November 11, 1861. His brother Dom Luiz, who has received a most liberal education, and is animated with the noblest aspirations for the welfare of his country, is zealous in carrying out the reforms planned by Pombal, which had been continually retarded by the frequent revolutions. The violent political agitations have at last come to an end, and the Portuguese nation, so long a prey to ignorance and egotistical passions, gradually resumes its proper place among the civilized nations of Europe.

PRESENT STATE OF EDUCATION IN PORTUGAL.

[NOTE.—For the following report on primary education in Portugal we are indebted to an article on this subject in *O Novo Mundo*, (April 23, 1873,) a monthly illustrated Portuguese journal, published in New York, and kindly forwarded to this Office by the editor, Mr. J. C. Rodrigues. In the brief account on secondary and special instruction we have chiefly followed Professor Le Roy's article in Schmid's *Educational Cyclopedia;* and also a report by the Brazilian minister at Lisbon, kindly forwarded to this Bureau by the Brazilian minister at Washington.]

PRIMARY EDUCATION.—COURSE OF INSTRUCTION.

The decree of September 20, 1844, divided primary instruction into two grades, prescribing the following course of instruction for the first grade: Reading, writing, arithmetic, elements of Christian doctrine and morality, grammatical exercises, principles of chorography and history of Portugal; and for the second grade: Portuguese grammar, linear drawing, general history and geography, sacred history, elementary arithmetic, elementary geometry. Recently the course of instruction in the first grade has been somewhat enlarged, transferring to it some of the studies of the second grade, penmanship, legal system of weights and measures, &c. It must be said that there is no general and well-defined programme for the elementary schools, and that the condition of the larger portion of the elementary schools of the kingdom is unsatisfactory, partly on account of the incapacity of the teachers, partly because the few schools which have good teachers want pupils, many parents keeping their children from school to assist them in their agricultural and industrial pursuits, so that few children learn more than to read badly and to write incorrectly. Thus the brutality and stupidity of the parents, and the culpable negligence of the government in permitting the law which imposes fines and even the loss of political rights on teachers neglecting their duty, and on parents who do not send their children between the ages of seven and fifteen years to school, to remain a dead letter, are the causes of the lamentable disproportion (one to sixteen) between the number of children attending school and the number that reach any degree of proficiency. The cause of the great ignorance of most of the teachers is obvious, and will remain so till the government pays them a better salary, as very few young men care to become teachers when they have the prospect of making an infinitely better living in almost any other profession or trade, while as teachers they see nothing before them but a life full of vexation and want.

ATTENDANCE AT SCHOOL.

During the scholastic year 1871–1872 the public elementary schools (day- and night-schools) had enrolled 113,097 children, viz, 92,834 boys and 20,263 girls; but only 52,190, viz, 41,599 boys and 10,591 girls, attended regularly; and at the end of the year only 7,107, viz, 5,919 boys and 1,188 girls, could receive the character "prompt in attendance." In comparing these figures with the last census of Portugal we arrive at the following deplorable result: Proportion of attendance to the male population, 1 to 50; and to the female population, 1 to 215. The scholastic year of ten months has about 230 school-days, approximately representing 1,440 school-hours for every primary school.

WANT OF GOOD TEXT-BOOKS.

The want of good elementary text-books is another cause of the little progress made in the public schools. There are no text-books officially adopted for primary instruction. The council of public instruction sanctions some every year, but leaves the choice out of a constantly increasing number to the teacher in every school. The same is the case with regard to the methods of instruction; each teacher follows the one which he prefers, and some follow no method whatever. This want of uniformity in the methods of public instruction shows itself even in the schools of one and the same city. Some teachers use the simultaneous method, others the mixed (mutual and simultaneous) method, and a few the so-called Portuguese method which the Viscount of Castilho endeavored to introduce in the country.

INSPECTION.

The inspection of schools, which in every country is acknowledged as essential for the organization of public instruction, is in the most miserable condition. There are in each of the twenty-one districts of the kingdom commissioners of education, whose duty it is to inspect the schools; but they do not exercise their power, nor are they able to do so, being almost all rectors or professors of national lyceums, receiving as commissioners only a very insignificant remuneration, scarcely sufficient to pay their traveling expenses, even if they should only undertake to visit the schools once a year. They are under the supervision of the respective political authorities, who, however, are generally not able to inspect the schools, and do not receive any instructions as regards such duties, and who, even if they wished to fulfill their duties in this respect, could only do so by neglecting their administrative duties. The result of all this is that, with rare exceptions, the public schools do not enable pupils to pass the examination in primary subjects which is required for admission to the lyceum. Of all the pupils marked "prompt" in the private school-examinations, not one in fifty is fit for the public examination of admission.

TEACHERS.

The salaries of teachers are wretched. Teachers for lifetime (*professores vitalicios*) receive 150 millreas in Lisbon, Oporto, and Funchal, (about $175,) and in other places 100 millreas. Temporary teachers receive 140 millreas in Lisbon, and 90 in other places. Teachers are obliged to keep school six hours per day five days each week. As a general rule school is held during day-time every week-day, except Thursdays and ecclesiastical holidays, in two sessions, one in the morning and one in the afternoon; but if local circumstances make it necessary, the school-hours may be transferred to the evening.

NIGHT-SCHOOLS.

There are in various places night-schools for adults, partly kept by the regular teacher of the public school, partly by private individuals. The Minister Marteno Ferrão was very active in creating this class of schools, and organized them by a regulation of November 28, 1867. As a general rule the night-schools are confined to the instruction of adults, only in exceptional cases boys younger than fourteen years are admitted. There are no night-schools for females. Those night-schools which are kept by the regular public-school teacher are free, and are in operation during the whole scholastic year, either three or five times per week. Teachers who keep night-schools are exempt from teaching one of the daily sessions, and receive a small remuneration either from the government, the district, or municipal authorities. Night-schools kept by private individuals are supported either by corporations or by private munificence. The total number of night-schools in the kingdom is about 580, with 7,000 scholars.

ESTABLISHMENT OF NEW SCHOOLS.

With regard to the establishment of new primary schools, the government is authorized to establish schools for both sexes, and in any locality, without consulting the legislative assembly, keeping in the limits, however, of the sum voted for the contingent expenses of primary instruction. The way of proceeding is briefly this: some town, or parish, or municipal authority wishing the establishment of a new school makes an application to the governor of the province, making at the same time the indispensable offer of a school-house and school-furniture, and also, if possible, books for poor scholars, rewards for diligent scholars, a dwelling-house for the teacher, &c. The governor refers the matter to the general council of public instruction, mentioning the local circumstances, the necessity for such a school, the probable number of pupils, &c. The consulting council gives its opinion, and if this is favorable, the executive decrees the establishment of the school, publishing it in the official journal, appoints a committee to see to it that all the conditions are fulfilled, and also to examine into the sanitary condition of the school-building. After this has been found to be satisfactory, a teacher is appointed, after a competitive examination, from the various applicants for the place. Candidates must be more than twenty years old, possess certificates of ability and good moral character, and must have satisfied the law of military service.

STATISTICS OF PRIMARY INSTRUCTION.

DISTRICTS.	SCHOOLS.			TEACHERS.			SCHOLARS.	
	For boys.	For girls.	Total.	Male.	Female.	Total.	Enrolled.	Regular in attendance.
Aveiro	122	18	140	122	18	140	8,155	2,620
Beja	53	11	64	53	11	64	3,661	898
Braga	106	11	117	106	11	117	7,769	3,219
Bragança	107	15	122	107	15	122	4,762	3,083
Castello Branco	91	16	107	91	16	107	4,784	1,939
Coimbra	129	19	148	129	19	148	7,506	4,095
Evora	40	9	49	40	9	49	2,520	1,363
Faro	46	4	50	46	4	50	2,638	850
Guarda	174	26	200	174	26	200	9,268	3,924
Leiria	77	11	88	77	11	88	3,421	2,308
Lisbon	135	46	181	137	46	183	10,557	6,450
Portalegre	52	12	64	52	12	64	1,313	654
Porto	131	28	159	131	28	159	9,422	5,646
Santarem	92	16	108	92	17	109	4,566	1,465
Vianna do Castello	83	5	88	83	5	88	5,943	3,327
Villa Real	142	21	163	142	21	163	6,862	3,470
Vizeu	222	29	251	222	29	251	12,021	2,655
Total of the continent	1,802	297	2,099	1,804	298	2,102	105,168	47,263
Angra	34	6	40	34	7	41	2,084	1,362
Funchal	24	9	33	24	9	33	1,377	653
Horta	29	13	42	29	13	42	2,615	1,876
Ponta Delgada	21	9	30	21	9	30	1,853	1,036
Total of the islands	108	37	145	108	38	146	7,929	4,927
Total of the kingdom	1,910	334	2,244	1,912	336	2,248	113,097	52,190

SECONDARY EDUCATION.

After the establishment of a constitutional government, secondary education in Portugal, which up to that time had been confined to the study of the Greek and Roman classics, took a new direction. It cannot be denied that all the political parties which succeeded each other in the government of this beautiful country were animated by the most laudable zeal for promoting the intellectual welfare of the people, and did all in their power to diffuse education in every part of the country. The condition of the political organization, and the varied interests springing from it, made a complete reform of all grades of public instruction more indispensable than ever.

The establishment of national lyceums in the capitals of the administrative districts tended greatly to the better development of secondary instruction by enlarging the course of instruction, and by introducing the elements of physical and mathematical sciences, of natural history, of the graphic arts, and their application to commerce, industry, and agriculture, thus realizing an eminently civilizing and liberal idea, as the Marquis de Avila e Bolame well remarked in a circular proposing a reform of the course of instruction. The national lyceums form in fact the weightiest element in the reformed system of general education. The institutions are frequented by all those who wish to prepare themselves for higher scientific studies, and by those who intend to devote themselves to more arduous labors, which, perfected by the light of science, are the essential conditions of the life and prosperity of modern society. It is acknowledged, however, that these institutions cannot well answer their true object so long as elementary education is so backward, and so long as there are no intermediate schools where pupils can study the first elements of literary and scientific knowledge, which, according to the natural development of the intellectual faculties, are to be perfected by secondary instruction, as the essential basis of a solid education, and not with the sole aim of forming the preparatory studies for the different spheres of public life. Superior instruction alone entitles a man to aspire to government offices, and the young men are led by by-paths through which they can in less time enter upon superior studies and obtain academic degrees. For this reason the secondary studies are gone through superficially, and sink down to the level of public instruction, producing, with rare exceptions, an incomplete and mechanical education, utterly prejudicial to those solid and thorough studies which alone constitute true mental culture. These facts were duly appreciated, and revealed the sore point in this system of public education, the inevitable decadence of secondary studies, which, reduced to simple preparatory instruction, could not contribute anything toward the moral and intellectual culture of the nation, toward true civilization and true liberty. In order that secondary instruction may reach this lofty aim, it is indispensable to make it truly useful, organizing it on a broad and solid basis, calculated for the general and harmonious culture of all the human faculties.

Literary education in Portugal is at present imparted by professional instruction; the sciences and their application hold their proper place in the course of instruction, and the national lyceums are the centers of this general education, so profitable to the individual and to society. Considering that scientific education would always be defective without the greatest possible amount of literary studies, and with a view of making the lyceums answer this twofold end, the number of lyceums has been limited to those absolutely necessary, establishing at the same time, by the side of the lyceums, courses of instruction where some of those subjects may be studied which are not taught in the lyceums.

It was thought indispensable to create academical districts, which might form the other great centers of the literary and scientific administration of the public and private establishments. Economical and other reasons determined the choice of these districts, and Lisbon, Oporto, and Coimbra, as centers of special and superior instruction, were designated as the seats of the three districts. The small revenue of the state requires the utmost parsimony in the public expenses, and this is the cause of the miserable salaries of the professors, who are the worst-paid class of public servants. The full liberty of teaching which exists in Portugal, has produced many private secondary schools, which keep up a strong emulation with the public schools. The course of instruction in the lyceums embraces the following subjects: Portuguese, Latin, arithmetic, geometry, elements of algebra, philosophy, morals, principles of natural law, rhetoric, classical and especially Portuguese literature, history, chronology, and geography. Some of the lyceums introduce also other subjects in their course; thus at Lisbon: Greek, Hebrew, French, English, Arabic, commercial sciences, applied mechanics; at Oporto: Greek, French, English, and German; at Braga and Evora: Greek, French, English, book-keeping; in Portalegre, Villa Real, and Castello Branco: agriculture, &c.

There are no recent statistics of secondary instruction; therefore the statistics of 1855 are given; according to these there were in the 20 lyceal districts 210 teachers, and 3,338 students.

SUPERIOR INSTRUCTION.

There is only one institution for superior instruction, viz, the University of Coimbra, which has five faculties, viz: 1. Theology; 2. Law; 3. Medicine, surgery, and pharmacy; 4. Mathematics; and 5. Philosophy, which means only natural sciences, physics, chemistry, &c.; as also agriculture, technology, and veterinary surgery. There are three degrees, viz: Baccalaureate, licentiate, and doctor.

University instruction in Coimbra, till quite recently, lacked life, and there never was a complete and harmonious group of lectures on the humanitarian sciences and philology, and on ancient and modern literature, such as the *faculté des lettres* in France. Till the year 1859, logic, morals, and metaphysics were confined to the lyceums, where the antiquated methods reigned supreme. When, impelled by the powerful influence of modern ideas, a young man emancipated himself and resisted the soporific influence of traditional methods, he would rather plunge into the whirlpool of political party agitation than employ his leisure to increase his knowledge and thus to become better able to grapple with the great questions of the day. There are some very honorable exceptions, but mostly of Portuguese who have studied in foreign countries. The enervating climate and the heat of revolutionary passions have doubtless contributed toward keeping up this turbulent, impatient spirit; but the Portuguese race has such a happy disposition, that there is every reason to hope for the best results from the reforms which have been introduced. In this conviction the late king, by a decree of June 8, 1859, founded at his own expense, in Lisbon, a sort of *faculté des lettres*. This higher college has five professorships: 1, Portuguese and universal history; 2, Greek and Latin literature; 3, modern European, especially Portuguese, literature; 4, philosophy; and 5, history of philosophy. The professors have equal rank with those of the University of Coimbra. After the two-years' course has been finished, there is an examination, and theses have to be defended, after which the successful candidates receive the diploma of *graduados em letras*, (graduates of literature.) This institution has exercised a beneficial influence on the University of Coimbra, and ancient and modern languages and literature are studied there more than formerly.

SPECIAL INSTRUCTION.

All the Portuguese special schools are officially classed under superior instruction. Prominent above all others is the Royal Polytechnic School at Lisbon, organized in 1779 under the name "Royal Naval Academy," reorganized by a decree of December 10, 1851, and since 1860 under the ministry of the interior, because it is intended as well for civil engineers as for military engineers and artillery officers. Scholars enter at the age of fourteen, after having passed a very rigorous examination in French, logic, linear drawing, arithmetic, elements of algebra, geometry, trigonometry, mathematical geography, elements of natural history, as likewise in all the elementary studies. The course of instruction lasts from three to four years, and during this time the military scholars, called "cadets," engage in practical exercises in that branch of the military service in which they are to serve. The school is under the direction of a lieutenant-colonel. There are eleven professorships, each with a professor and an assistant professor, viz, mathematics, mechanics, surveying, astronomy, physics and chemistry, geology, mineralogy and metallurgy, botany and agriculture, zoology and comparative physiology, political economy, and commercial and administrative law. Connected with the school there is a library and a well-arranged museum of natural history.

The polytechnic academy at Oporto is at the same time a naval school, a business college, and a higher school of arts and trades. It has nineteen professors and assistants.

There is no school of mining, but mining engineers study at foreign schools, and the government allows every year at least three to study at the public expense.

Portugal possesses ten agricultural schools of different grades, viz, six instruction-farms in the country, three district-schools, in Lisbon, Evora, and Coimbra, and finally the Normal-School of Agriculture in Lisbon, connected with the district-school in that city, under whose supervision there is since 1853 the botanical garden at Ajuda. Every district-school has a model-farm, the revenues from which belong to the proprietor, and which is managed by him with a special view to agricultural instruction. The government pays him a fixed salary, and furnishes an assistant. There are ten free places in every district-school. Students enter at the age of sixteen years, and the course of instruction lasts three years; in the normal institute at Lisbon it lasts five years.

There are two institutions for art and industry, one in Lisbon, founded

5 E

in 1836, and united with the polytechnic school in 1844, with twelve professors and assistants, and one in Oporto, connected with the polytechnic academy, with eight professors and assistants. There are in these institutions, among the rest, courses of historical painting, anatomy, optics, perspective, &c.